Longman School
Shakespeare

Romeo and Juliet

John O'Connor, Volume Editor
Beth Wood, Activity Writer
Margaret Graham, Consultant

John O'Connor, Editor
Dr Stewart Eames, Textual Consultant

KU-525-721

PEARSON
Longman

Pearson Education Limited
Edinburgh Gate
Harlow
Essex
CM20 2JE
England
and Associated Companies throughout the World

3wK

822.33ROM

4,50

ISBN 0582 848741

Printed in China
SWTC/01

First published 2004

The Publisher's policy is to use paper manufactured from sustainable forests.

We are grateful to the following for permission to reproduce copyright
photographs:

ArenaPAL pages 126 bottom, 127 top, 191 bottom; Catherine Ashmore
pages 12 bottom, 97 top, 257 top, 261; Laurence Burns pages 13 bottom,
15 bottom, 37, 126 top; Nobby Clark pages 97 bottom, 127 bottom, 222
top; Joe Cocks Studio Collection/Shakespeare Birthplace Trust pages 146 top,
258, 259; Donald Cooper pages 2, 3, 4, 8 bottom, 9, 11, 13 top, 14 bottom,
36, 74 bottom, 75, 104 top, 105, 146 bottom, 147 top, 190, 191 top, 222
bottom, 223, 256, 263; Ronald Grant Archive pages 8 top, 10, 12 top, 14
top, 104 bottom, 257 bottom, 267; Image Bank/Andre Pistolesi
page 265; Robbie Jack page 96; 20th Century Fox/The Kobal
Collection/Morton, Merrick pages 74 top, 147 bottom; Richard Mildenhall
page 15 top; Paramount/The Kobal Collection page 269.

Cover photograph: Getty Images/Stone (Darren Robb)

Picture researcher: Louise Edgeworth

ACT 1: SCENE BY SCENE

The Chorus sets the scene in Verona and outlines the story of the two lovers.

1 Benvolio tries to stop a fight between Capulet and Montague servants, but is attacked by Tybalt. The Prince threatens the death penalty if the families disturb the streets in this way ever again. Romeo has been unhappy, and his parents, Lord and Lady Montague, discuss this with Benvolio. Romeo reveals to Benvolio that he is in love, but that the girl is rejecting him.

2 Capulet agrees to allow Paris to woo his daughter, Juliet. Learning that Rosaline, the girl Romeo loves, is to be a guest at the Capulet ball, Benvolio suggests that they gate-crash it.

3 Lady Capulet tells Juliet of Paris's request to marry her and Juliet agrees to consider Paris as a possible husband.

4 Romeo is worried about going to the Capulet ball because of a troubling dream. Mercutio says that the dream was only caused by Queen Mab, who comes to people in their sleep and gives them strange fantasies.

5 Tybalt is angry that Romeo has gate-crashed the ball and threatens revenge. Romeo meets Juliet and they fall in love, but both are later dismayed to learn that they are from rival families.

ACT 2: SCENE BY SCENE

The Chorus talks about the difficulties that Romeo and Juliet will have to overcome.

1 Leaving the party, Romeo hides from his friends and refuses to come when Mercutio calls him.

2 Hiding inside the Capulet's garden, Romeo sees Juliet at a window and hears her declare her love for him. They express their love for one another and Juliet asks Romeo to send a message the next day telling her when and where they can be married.

3 Romeo visits Friar Lawrence. When Romeo tells him about Juliet, he agrees to marry them because it might help to heal the bitterness between the feuding families.

4 Benvolio tells Mercutio that Romeo has been sent a challenge to a duel by Tybalt, a dangerous fighter. Juliet's Nurse arrives and Romeo asks her to tell Juliet to meet him that afternoon, when the Friar will marry them.

5 When the Nurse finally returns to an impatient Juliet, she passes on Romeo's instructions.

6 Friar Lawrence warns Romeo about the danger of his sudden love for Juliet, but agrees to marry the lovers in secret.

ACT 3: SCENE BY SCENE

1 Tybalt comes looking for Romeo, determined to get revenge. When they meet, Romeo refuses to fight him. Angry with Romeo for putting up with Tybalt's insults, Mercutio challenges Tybalt himself and is fatally wounded. To get revenge for the dead Mercutio, Romeo kills Tybalt and then flees. The Prince banishes him from Verona.

2 When the Nurse reports that Romeo has killed Tybalt, Juliet grieves for him, but is also distraught at Romeo's banishment. She asks the Nurse to bring Romeo to her.

3 The Friar unsuccessfully tries to comfort Romeo, who is devastated at being banished. The Nurse arrives to tell him that Juliet wants to see him before he leaves.

4 Capulet tells Paris that Juliet is mourning for Tybalt, but decides that she will marry Paris in three days' time.

5 At dawn the next day, Juliet makes Romeo leave before he is captured. When told that she is to marry Paris, Juliet refuses and her father angrily threatens to throw her out unless she agrees. The Nurse advises her to go through with the marriage to Paris, but Juliet plans to seek help from the Friar.

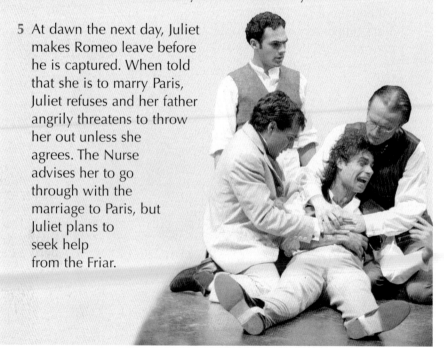

ACT 4: SCENE BY SCENE

1 Juliet sees Paris at the Friar's cell. Realising how desperate Juliet is, the Friar suggests Juliet take a potion to make her seem dead. The Friar will write to Romeo and arrange for him to collect Juliet when she wakes in the Capulet tomb.

2 On the Friar's advice, Juliet apologises to her father and pretends to agree to marry Paris the following day.

3 Despite imagining the horrors of what might go wrong, Juliet drinks the potion.

4 Hearing Paris arriving for the wedding, Capulet orders that Juliet should be woken up.

5 The Nurse finds Juliet apparently dead. The Friar tries to comfort the mourners as plans are made for her funeral.

ACT 5: SCENE BY SCENE

1 In Mantua, Balthasar tells Romeo that Juliet is dead. Deciding to join Juliet in the tomb that night, Romeo buys poison and leaves for Verona.

2 Friar Lawrence learns that the letter he had sent to Romeo has not been delivered. He rushes off to the tomb.

3 At the Capulet tomb, Romeo is challenged by Paris. They fight, and Paris is killed. Romeo looks at Juliet for the last time, kisses her and drinks the poison. Friar Lawrence enters to find Romeo dead. When Juliet wakes, the Friar tries to explain what has happened, but flees when he hears people approaching. Juliet kisses Romeo and stabs herself. The Friar, under arrest, explains to the Prince what has happened. In their grief, Capulet and Montague make peace.

THE HOUSE OF CAPULET

CAPULET
Juliet's father
He promises Paris that
Juliet can marry him.

LADY CAPULET
Juliet's mother
She supports her
husband when Juliet
refuses to marry Paris.

COUSIN CAPULET
Capulet's older cousin
A guest at the feast.

JULIET
*Capulet's 14-year-old
daughter*
She falls in love with
Romeo and marries him
in secret.

TYBALT
Juliet's cousin
He kills Mercutio and is
then himself killed by
Romeo.

NURSE
*Juliet's nurse since she
was a baby*
She helps Juliet to marry
Romeo in secret.

PETER
The Nurse's servant
He goes with the Nurse
when she meets Romeo.

SAMPSON AND GREGORY
Servants
They fight with the
Montagues in the brawl.

SERVANT
He cannot read and asks
Romeo to tell him who
is on the guest list for
the feast.

THE PRINCE'S FAMILY

ESCALUS
Prince of Verona
He banishes Romeo
for killing Tybalt.

MERCUTIO
A relative of the Prince
He is Romeo's friend and
is killed by Tybalt.

COUNT PARIS
A relative of the Prince
Capulet arranges for him
to marry Juliet.

The House of Montague

MONTAGUE
Romeo's father

LADY MONTAGUE
Romeo's mother
She dies of grief when
Romeo is banished.

ROMEO
Montague's son
He falls in love with Juliet
and secretly marries her,
but is banished when he
kills Tybalt.

BENVOLIO
Romeo's cousin and friend
He has to report to the
Prince how Romeo came
to kill Tybalt.

BALTHASAR
Romeo's servant
He takes news to Romeo
when he is banished to
Mantua.

ABRAHAM
Servant
He is involved in the
brawl with the Capulets.

Others in Verona

FRIAR LAWRENCE
A priest and Romeo's friend
He secretly marries Romeo
and Juliet, and tries to help
Juliet avoid marrying Paris.

FRIAR JOHN
Another priest
He is prevented from
delivering Friar Lawrence's
letter to Romeo in Mantua.

MUSICIANS
They are hired to play at
the wedding of Juliet and
Paris.

WATCHMEN
Paris's page fetches them
when Romeo and Paris
fight at the Capulet tomb.

In Mantua

AN APOTHECARY
A poor pharmacist
He sells poison to Romeo.

Romeo and Juliet, 1996 (directed by B. Luhrmann)

Shakespeare's Globe, 2004

RSC, 1997

RSC, 2004

Romeo and Juliet, 1996 (directed by B. Luhrmann)

RSC, 1980

Shakespeare's Globe, 2004

Düsseldorfer Schauspielhaus, 1994

Romeo and Juliet, 1996 (directed by B. Luhrmann)

National Theatre, 2000

RSC, 1995

RSC, 1986

Romeo and Juliet, 1996 (directed by B. Luhrmann)

RSC, 1995

RSC, 1991

RSC, 1986

CHARACTER LIST

THE CHORUS

THE HOUSE OF CAPULET

CAPULET

LADY CAPULET

JULIET *their daughter*

TYBALT *Juliet's cousin*

Juliet's **NURSE**

Capulet's **SERVANT**

PETER *the Nurse's servant*

an old **COUSIN**

SAMPSON *a servant*

GREGORY *a servant*

Tybalt's **PAGE**

other **SERVANTS** *and* **FOLLOWERS**

THE HOUSE OF MONTAGUE

MONTAGUE

LADY MONTAGUE

ROMEO *their son*

BENVOLIO *Romeo's friend*

BALTHASAR *Romeo's servant*

ABRAHAM *a servant*

other **SERVANTS**

THE PRINCE'S FAMILY

    PRINCE ESCALUS *of Verona*

    MERCUTIO *a relative of the Prince*

    COUNT PARIS *another relative*

    Paris's **PAGE**

    Mercutio's **PAGE**

    ATTENDANTS *and* **GUARDS**

ALSO FROM VERONA

    FRIAR LAWRENCE *a Franciscan friar*

    FRIAR JOHN *his friend*

    an **OFFICER**

    Men of the **WATCH**

    MUSICIANS

    GUESTS *at the Capulet feast*

    CITIZENS

IN MANTUA

    an **APOTHECARY**

Scenes are set in Verona, except for Act 5 Scene 1, which takes place in Mantua.

The Chorus introduces the story, set in Verona. A long-standing feud between the Montague and Capulet families will be ended only by the deaths of the lovers, Romeo and Juliet.

1 **households**: families
both ... dignity: as noble as each other
3 **ancient grudge**: long-term hatred
mutiny: outburst of violence
4 **civil blood**: i.e. citizens' injuries and deaths
5 **From ... foes**: born from these two enemies, lethal to one another
6 **star-crossed**: ill-fated
7 **misadventured**: pitiful and tragic
overthrows: downfalls
8 **strife**: feud
9 **passage**: course
death-marked: doomed to death
11 **but ... end**: except for the deaths of their children
12 **traffic**: business
14 **What ... mend**: i.e. the actors' hard work will try to make up for any weaknesses in their performance of the play

---

Think about

• The Prologue is written in the form of a sonnet (a fourteen-line poem often divided into sections/ quatrains). How are the first three sections (lines 1 to 4, 5 to 8, and 9 to 12) used to introduce the performance?

Enter CHORUS.

CHORUS   Two households, both alike in dignity,
          In fair Verona where we lay our scene,
          From ancient grudge break to new mutiny,
          Where civil blood makes civil hands unclean.
          From forth the fatal loins of these two foes   5
          A pair of star-crossed lovers take their life;
          Whose misadventured piteous overthrows
          Doth with their death bury their parents' strife.
          The fearful passage of their death-marked love,
          And the continuance of their parents' rage,   10
          Which, but their children's end, nought could remove,
          Is now the two hours' traffic of our stage –
              The which, if you with patient ears attend,
              What here shall miss, our toil shall strive to mend.

                                                          Exit.

In this scene ...

- A street fight breaks out between the Capulets and the Montagues.
- The Prince stops the riot and threatens the death penalty for anyone caught fighting in Verona's streets again.
- Romeo's parents ask Benvolio why Romeo has been behaving strangely.
- Romeo tells Benvolio that he is in love with a girl who refuses to be won over.

Two Capulet servants, Sampson and Gregory, brag about their part in the feud with the Montagues.

Think about

- What are Sampson and Gregory boasting about (lines 1 to 27)? What do you think this might have to do with the rest of the play?

- Lines 1 to 4 contain wordplay: to 'carry coals' is to be humiliated, 'colliers' (coal-miners) were considered dirty and dishonest, 'choler' (pronounced 'collar') means anger, and a 'collar' was also a hangman's noose. Why might some directors cut these jokes in a performance? Why might others decide to keep them?

s.d. **bucklers**: small shields
1 **carry coals**: i.e. do work that is below us
2 **colliers**: coal-miners
3 **choler**: anger
   draw: i.e. draw our swords
4 **draw ... collar**: i.e. avoid hanging
5 **moved**: made angry

8 **stand**: i.e. fight

11 **take the wall**: walk where the road is cleanest, i.e. show my superiority
12–13 **goes to the wall**: is defeated by the strong
14–15 **weaker vessels**: 'the weaker sex'

19 **'Tis all one**: It makes no difference

23 **maidenheads**: virginities

25 **They must ... it**: The ones who sense it are the ones who feel it (i.e. the maids)

A street in Verona.

Enter SAMPSON *and* GREGORY *(servants of the house of*
Capulet), armed with swords and bucklers.

SAMPSON	Gregory, on my word, we'll not carry coals.	
GREGORY	No, for then we should be colliers.	
SAMPSON	I mean, an we be in choler, we'll draw.	
GREGORY	Ay, while you live, draw your neck out of collar.	
SAMPSON	I strike quickly, being moved.	5
GREGORY	But thou art not quickly moved to strike.	
SAMPSON	A dog of the house of Montague moves me.	
GREGORY	To move is to stir, and to be valiant is to stand: therefore, if thou art moved thou runn'st away.	
SAMPSON	A dog of that house shall move me to stand. I will take the wall of any man or maid of Montague's.	10
GREGORY	That shows thee a weak slave, for the weakest goes to the wall.	
SAMPSON	'Tis true, and therefore women, being the weaker vessels, are ever thrust to the wall: therefore I will push Montague's men from the wall, and thrust his maids to the wall.	15
GREGORY	The quarrel is between our masters, and us their men.	
SAMPSON	'Tis all one. I will show myself a tyrant. When I have fought with the men, I will be civil with the maids: I will cut off their heads.	20
GREGORY	The heads of the maids?	
SAMPSON	Ay, the heads of the maids, or their maidenheads – take it in what sense thou wilt.	
GREGORY	They must take it in sense that feel it.	25

Two Montague servants approach. The Capulets try to start a fight.

29   **poor-John**: cheap dried fish
     tool: weapon

31   **naked weapon**: unsheathed sword

33   **Fear me not**: Have no fears about me

34   **marry**: indeed ('by the Virgin Mary')

35   **take ... sides**: have the law on our side

36   **list**: like

37   **bite my thumb**: make an insulting gesture

48   **I am for you**: i.e. I am ready to fight you

Think about

• The dialogue in lines 1 to 31 is full of sexual innuendoes (double-meanings). They include: 'stir' (have sex), 'stand' (have an erection), 'thrust', 'pretty piece of flesh' and 'tool'. What does this language tell you about Sampson and Gregory?

SAMPSON	Me they shall feel while I am able to stand – and 'tis known I am a pretty piece of flesh.
GREGORY	'Tis well thou art not fish: if thou hadst, thou hadst been poor-John. Draw thy tool – here comes two of the house of Montagues.

30

Enter ABRAHAM *and* BALTHASAR *(servants of the house of Montague).*

SAMPSON	My naked weapon is out. Quarrel! I will back thee.
GREGORY	How? Turn thy back and run?
SAMPSON	Fear me not.
GREGORY	No, marry. I fear *thee*!
SAMPSON	Let us take the law of our sides: let them begin.

35

GREGORY	I will frown as I pass by, and let them take it as they list.
SAMPSON	Nay, as they dare. I will bite my thumb at them, which is disgrace to them if they bear it.
ABRAHAM	Do you bite your thumb at us, sir?
SAMPSON	I do bite my thumb, sir.

40

ABRAHAM	Do you bite your thumb at *us*, sir?
SAMPSON	*(Aside to* GREGORY) Is the law of our side if I say 'Ay'?
GREGORY	*(Aside to* SAMPSON) No.
SAMPSON	No, sir, I do not bite my thumb at you, sir, but I bite my thumb, sir.

45

GREGORY	Do you quarrel, sir?
ABRAHAM	Quarrel, sir? No, sir.
SAMPSON	But if you do, sir, I am for you. I serve as good a man as you.
ABRAHAM	No better.

50

SAMPSON	Well, sir –

Sampson and Gregory grow
bolder when Tybalt, a Capulet,
arrives, and the fight begins.
Benvolio, a Montague, tries to
stop them, but it quickly turns
into a public brawl.

56 **swashing**: slashing

59 **Put up**: Sheathe your swords

60 **heartless hinds**: 1 servants lacking
courage; 2 female deer without male
protection

63 **manage**: use
part: separate

Think about

- What impression do you get
of Tybalt from his first
appearance?

- If you were the director,
how would you want the
Montague servants and
Benvolio to react when
Tybalt arrives (line 59)?

- What are your first
impressions of Capulet?

67 **bills**: long-handled axes
partisans: spears

69 **long sword**: heavy, old-fashioned
weapon

72 **spite**: defiance

Enter BENVOLIO.

GREGORY   (*Aside to* SAMPSON) Say 'better'! – Here comes one of my master's kinsmen.

SAMPSON   (*To* ABRAHAM) Yes – better, sir.

ABRAHAM   You lie!   55

SAMPSON   Draw, if you be men! Gregory, remember thy swashing blow!

They fight.

BENVOLIO *draws his sword and tries to separate them.*

BENVOLIO   Part, fools!
          Put up your swords! You know not what you do.

Enter TYBALT.

TYBALT   What, art thou drawn among these heartless hinds?   60
          Turn thee, Benvolio! Look upon thy death.

BENVOLIO   I do but keep the peace! Put up thy sword
          Or manage it to part these men with me.

TYBALT   What, drawn, and talk of peace? I hate the word
          As I hate hell, all Montagues, and thee.   65
          Have at thee, coward!

They fight.

Enter a city OFFICER, *with three or four armed citizens, who rush in to try to stop the fighting.*

OFFICER   Clubs, bills and partisans! Strike! Beat them down!
          Down with the Capulets! Down with the Montagues!

Enter old CAPULET, *in his dressing-gown, followed by* LADY CAPULET, *his wife.*

CAPULET   What noise is this? Give me my long sword, ho!

LADY CAPULET   A crutch, a crutch! Why call you for a sword?   70

CAPULET   My sword I say! Old Montague is come,
          And flourishes his blade in spite of me!

The Prince of Verona speaks angrily to Montague and Capulet. He threatens the death penalty for anyone caught fighting on the streets again. Montague asks Benvolio how the fighting began.

76 **Profaners**: mis-users
neighbour-stainèd steel: swords, stained with your neighbours' blood

78 **quench**: put out
pernicious: destructive

81 **mistempered**: 1 angry; 2 made for use in a bad cause

82 **movèd**: angry

83 **civil brawls**: public riots
airy word: trivial comment

87 **cast**: throw down
grave ... ornaments: staffs etc., fitting for their age and status

89 **Cankered**: i.e. rusty
cankered hate: cancerous hatred

91 **Your lives ... peace**: i.e. you will be executed, for having broken the peace

95 **our farther pleasure**: what else I decide to do

98 **set ... abroach**: opened up this old quarrel

100 **adversary**: enemy

101 **ere**: before

103 **prepared**: already drawn

Think about

• What threat does the Prince make to Montague and Capulet? Why might this be important later in the play?

• What do you think of the Prince's statements? Do you think he is being firm enough, for example?

Enter old MONTAGUE *and* LADY MONTAGUE, *his wife.*

MONTAGUE   Thou villain, Capulet! (*To his wife*) Hold me not – let
                me go!

LADY MONTAGUE Thou shalt not stir one foot to seek a foe.

Enter PRINCE ESCALUS *(ruler of Verona), with guards and
attendants.*

PRINCE   Rebellious subjects, enemies to peace,   75
                Profaners of this neighbour-stainèd steel –
                Will they not hear? What ho! You men, you beasts,
                That quench the fire of your pernicious rage
                With purple fountains issuing from your veins!
                On pain of torture, from those bloody hands   80
                Throw your mistempered weapons to the ground,
                And hear the sentence of your movèd Prince.
                ⸂Three civil brawls bred of an airy word⸃
                By thee, old Capulet, and Montague,
                Have thrice disturbed the quiet of our streets,   85
                And made Verona's ancient citizens
                Cast by their grave beseeming ornaments
                To wield old partisans in hands as old,
                Cankered with peace, to part your cankered hate.
                If ever you disturb our streets again,   90
                Your lives shall pay the forfeit of the peace!
                For this time, all the rest depart away.
                You, Capulet, shall go along with me,
                And Montague, come you this afternoon,
                To know our farther pleasure in this case,   95
                To old Freetown, our common judgement-place.
                Once more, on pain of death, all men depart!

All exit, except MONTAGUE, LADY MONTAGUE, *and* BENVOLIO.

MONTAGUE   Who set this ancient quarrel new abroach?
                Speak, nephew. Were you by when it began?

BENVOLIO   Here were the servants of your adversary   100
                And yours, close fighting ere I did approach.
                I drew to part them. In the instant came
                The fiery Tybalt, with his sword prepared,
                Which, as he breathed defiance to my ears,

Benvolio, Montague and Lady Montague discuss Romeo's recent behaviour. He has been keeping to himself and seems depressed.

106 **nothing hurt withal**: not at all hurt by his strokes

108 **on ... part**: some on one side, some on the other

109 **either part**: both sides

111 **Right**: Very
fray: brawl

114 **abroad**: outside

116 **rooteth**: grows

118 **ware**: 1 aware; 2 wary
119 **stole ... covert**: crept into the shadows
120 **measuring his affections**: judging his feelings
121 **most sought ... found**: wanted most of all to be alone
122 **Being ... self**: my own company being too much for me
123 **my humour**: what I wanted
124 **shunned**: kept away from
126 **augmenting**: adding to

130 **Aurora**: goddess of the dawn
131 **heavy**: sad
132 **pens**: shuts

135 **portentous**: ominous
humour: moody behaviour
136 **counsel**: advice

138 **of**: from

139 **importuned**: tried to question

141 **his own ... counsellor**: discussing his feelings only with himself

Think about

- What are the first things we learn about Romeo (lines 112 to 136)? Why are Benvolio and Montague so concerned about him?

28

	He swung about his head and cut the winds,	105
	Who, nothing hurt withal, hissed him in scorn.	
	While we were interchanging thrusts and blows,	
	Came more and more, and fought on part and part,	
	Till the Prince came, who parted either part.	

LADY MONTAGUE O where is Romeo? Saw you him today?   110
               Right glad I am he was not at this fray.

BENVOLIO   Madam, an hour before the worshipped sun
               Peered forth the golden window of the east,
               A troubled mind drove me to walk abroad –
               Where, underneath the grove of sycamore   115
               That westward rooteth from this city side,
               So early walking did I see your son.
               Towards him I made, but he was ware of me,
               And stole into the covert of the wood.
               I, measuring his affections by my own,   120
               Which then most sought where most might not be found,
               Being one too many by my weary self,
               Pursued my humour not pursuing his,
               And gladly shunned who gladly fled from me.

MONTAGUE   Many a morning hath he there been seen,   125
               With tears augmenting the fresh morning's dew,
               Adding to clouds more clouds with his deep sighs.
               But all so soon as the all-cheering sun
               Should in the farthest east begin to draw
               The shady curtains from Aurora's bed,   130
               Away from light steals home my heavy son,
               And private in his chamber pens himself,
               Shuts up his windows, locks fair daylight out,
               And makes himself an artificial night.
               Black and portentous must this humour prove,   135
               Unless good counsel may the cause remove.

BENVOLIO   My noble uncle, do you know the cause?

MONTAGUE   I neither know it, nor can learn of him.

BENVOLIO   Have you importuned him by any means?

MONTAGUE   Both by myself and many other friends: 140
               But he, his own affections' counsellor,

Benvolio promises to try to discover the reason behind Romeo's unhappiness, and Montague and Lady Montague leave. Romeo admits to Benvolio that he is in love.

142 **true**: trustworthy
143 **close**: secretive
144 **sounding**: being worked out
145 **envious**: intending harm

150 **So please you**: If you please
151 **his grievance**: what's the matter with him
152 **I would ... stay**: I hope that, by staying here, you will be fortunate enough
153 **shrift**: confession (given to a priest)

Think about

• Shakespeare often uses imagery from the world of nature. What does the 'bud' image (lines 145 to 147) in Montague's speech tell us about Romeo's behaviour?

---

162 **Out ... love**: I love her, but she doesn't love me
163 **so gentle ... view**: which looks so pleasant
164 **tyrannous ... proof**: difficult when we experience it
165 **muffled**: Cupid was blindfolded.
166 **pathways ... will**: ways to get what he wants

Is to himself – I will not say how true –
But to himself so secret and so close,
So far from sounding and discovery
As is the bud bit with an envious worm   145
Ere he can spread his sweet leaves to the air,
Or dedicate his beauty to the sun.
Could we but learn from whence his sorrows grow,
We would as willingly give cure as know.

Enter ROMEO.

BENVOLIO   See where he comes. So please you, step aside.   150
              I'll know his grievance or be much denied.

MONTAGUE   I would thou wert so happy by thy stay
              To hear true shrift. Come, madam, let's away.

                    Exit MONTAGUE, *with* LADY MONTAGUE.

BENVOLIO   Good morrow, cousin.

ROMEO   Is the day so young?

BENVOLIO   But new struck nine.

ROMEO   Ay me, sad hours seem long.   155
              Was that my father that went hence so fast?

BENVOLIO   It was. What sadness lengthens Romeo's hours?

ROMEO   Not having that which, having, makes them short.

BENVOLIO   In love?

ROMEO   Out –   160

BENVOLIO   Of love?

ROMEO   Out of her favour where I am in love.

BENVOLIO   Alas, that Love, so gentle in his view,
              Should be so tyrannous and rough in proof!

ROMEO   Alas, that Love, whose view is muffled still,   165
              Should without eyes see pathways to his will!
              Where shall we dine? O me! What fray was here?
              Yet tell me not, for I have heard it all.
              Here's much to do with hate, but more with love.

Benvolio asks who the girl is, but Romeo does not tell him.

171 **of nothing ... create**: created out of nothing in the first place

172 **serious vanity**: weighty emptiness

173 **well-seeming**: attractive

175 **Still-waking**: always awake

176 **that ... this**: but am not loved in return

177 **coz**: cousin

178 **oppression**: unhappiness

179 **transgression**: offence / overstepping the limit

181 **propagate**: increase
     pressed: oppressed

185 **purged**: cleansed

186 **vexed**: troubled

187 **discreet**: cautious / sensitive

188 **gall**: bitter-tasting poison

189 **Soft**: Not so fast

193 **in sadness**: seriously

195 **sadly**: can also mean 'seriously'

199 **aimed so near**: guessed as much

Think about

- Romeo's speech (from line 169) is based on opposites and contains many oxymorons (expressions which seem to contradict themselves), such as 'loving hate'. These are often found in Elizabethan love-poetry. What others are there? What do they suggest about Romeo's state of mind?

Why then, O brawling love, O loving hate,   **170**
O anything of nothing first create!
O heavy lightness, serious vanity,
Misshapen chaos of well-seeming forms!
Feather of lead, bright smoke, cold fire, sick health,
Still-waking sleep, that is not what it is!   **175**
This love feel I, that feel no love in this.
Dost thou not laugh?

BENVOLIO   No, coz, I rather weep.

ROMEO   Good heart, at what?

BENVOLIO   At *thy* good heart's oppression.

ROMEO   Why, such is love's transgression.
Griefs of mine own lie heavy in my breast,   **180**
Which thou wilt propagate to have it pressed
With more of thine. This love that thou hast shown
Doth add more grief to too much of mine own.
Love is a smoke made with the fume of sighs:
Being purged, a fire sparkling in lovers' eyes;   **185**
Being vexed, a sea nourished with loving tears.
What is it else? A madness most discreet,
A choking gall, and a preserving sweet.
Farewell, my coz.

BENVOLIO   Soft, I will go along –
And if you leave me so, you do me wrong.   **190**

ROMEO   Tut, I have lost myself. I am not here.
This is not Romeo: he's some other where.

BENVOLIO   Tell me in sadness, who is that you love?

ROMEO   What, shall I groan and tell thee?

BENVOLIO   Groan? Why no –
But sadly tell me who.   **195**

ROMEO   Bid a sick man in sadness make his will –
A word ill urged to one that is so ill.
In sadness, cousin, I do love a woman.

BENVOLIO   I aimed so near when I supposed you loved.

Romeo says that the girl cannot be won over. He rejects Benvolio's suggestion that he should forget her and look at other girls.

200 mark-man: marksman / skilful archer

201 right fair mark: good target

203 Dian's wit: i.e. the good sense to avoid love (Diana was the Roman goddess of hunting and virginity)

204 proof: armour
chastity: sexual purity

205 uncharmed: i.e. unaffected by love's spell

206 will … terms: i.e. rejects love-talk

207 bide … eyes: accept loving glances

208 ope … gold: accept money

210 her store: i.e. her treasury of beauty

211 still: always

212 in that sparing: by saving herself

214 Cuts … posterity: i.e. her beauty will not be handed on to her children

216 merit bliss: i.e. go to heaven for her sexual purity

217 forsworn to: sworn that she will not

Think about

• The wordplay between Romeo and Benvolio (lines 199 to 203), starting with the expression 'I aimed so near', is based on archery. How does it build up from there? Who is Cupid and how does he fit in?

• What does Romeo's language in lines 202 to 210 suggest about his attitude to the girl?

223 call … more: think about her excellent beauty even more

228 passing fair: exceedingly attractive

230 passed: surpassed / exceeded

232 pay that doctrine: teach you that lesson
else … debt: i.e. I won't have done what I owe you as a friend

ROMEO	A right good mark-man! And she's fair I love.

200

BENVOLIO	A right fair mark, fair coz, is soonest hit.

ROMEO   Well, in that hit you miss. She'll not be hit
With Cupid's arrow. She hath Dian's wit,
And in strong proof of chastity well-armed,
From Love's weak childish bow she lives uncharmed.   **205**
She will not stay the siege of loving terms,
Nor bide th' encounter of assailing eyes,
Nor ope her lap to saint-seducing gold.
O, she is rich in beauty – only poor
That when she dies, with beauty dies her store.   **210**

BENVOLIO   Then she hath sworn that she will still live chaste?

ROMEO   She hath, and in that sparing makes huge waste,
For beauty, starved with her severity,
Cuts beauty off from all posterity.
She is too fair, too wise, wisely too fair,   **215**
To merit bliss by making me despair.
She hath forsworn to love, and in that vow
Do I live dead, that live to tell it now.

BENVOLIO   Be ruled by me: forget to think of her.

ROMEO   O, teach me how I should forget to think!   **220**

BENVOLIO   By giving liberty unto thine eyes:
Examine other beauties.

ROMEO   'Tis the way
To call hers – exquisite – in question more.
These happy masks that kiss fair ladies' brows,
Being black, puts us in mind they hide the fair.   **225**
He that is strucken blind cannot forget
The precious treasure of his eyesight lost.
Show me a mistress that is passing fair:
What doth her beauty serve, but as a note
Where I may read who passed that passing fair?   **230**
Farewell. Thou canst not teach me to forget.

BENVOLIO   I'll pay that doctrine, or else die in debt.

Exeunt.

35

RSC, 1995

RSC, 1986

37

In this scene ...

• Count Paris asks Capulet for his permission to woo Juliet.
• Benvolio persuades Romeo to go to the Capulet feast, where he can see girls who are more beautiful than the one he loves.

Count Paris wants to marry Juliet and asks her father for his consent. Capulet at first says that Juliet is too young to marry. But he agrees to let Paris woo her and he invites him to a feast at his house that evening.

Think about

• What impression have you formed of Capulet from this opening conversation? What is his attitude to Juliet getting married?

• How old is Juliet? Which of Capulet's comments tells us that she is an only child? Think why these facts might be important.

---

1 **bound**: ordered to keep the peace
2 **In ... alike**: or will face the same punishment

4 **reckoning**: reputation
5 **at odds**: as enemies
6 **suit**: request

7 **But saying o'er:** Simply repeating
8 **stranger**: newcomer

11 **Ere**: before

13 **marred**: spoiled

15 **hopeful ... earth**: 1 hope which forms the centre of my world; 2 lady who will inherit my wealth
18 **she agreed**: if she consents
19 **according**: agreeing

22 **store**: number

26 **comfort**: happiness
27 **well-apparelled**: i.e. clothed in flowers and leaves
30 **Inherit**: i.e. enjoy / experience
32 **mine**: i.e. my daughter
33 **stand in number**: be counted as one of the group
     in reckoning none: not high on your list

Another street.

Enter CAPULET, *Count* PARIS, *and Capulet's* SERVANT.

CAPULET	But Montague is bound as well as I,
	In penalty alike, and 'tis not hard, I think,
	For men so old as we to keep the peace.
PARIS	Of honourable reckoning are you both,
	And pity 'tis you lived at odds so long. 5
	But now, my lord, what say you to my suit?
CAPULET	But saying o'er what I have said before:
	My child is yet a stranger in the world;
	She hath not seen the change of fourteen years.
	Let two more summers wither in their pride 10
	Ere we may think her ripe to be a bride.
PARIS	Younger than she are happy mothers made.
CAPULET	And too soon marred are those so early made.
	Earth hath swallowed all my hopes but she.
	She is the hopeful lady of my earth. 15
	But woo her, gentle Paris, get her heart –
	My will to her consent is but a part.
	And she agreed, within her scope of choice
	Lies my consent and fair according voice.
	This night I hold an old accustomed feast, 20
	Whereto I have invited many a guest,
	Such as I love – and you among the store,
	One more most welcome, makes my number more.
	At my poor house look to behold this night
	Earth-treading stars that make dark heaven light. 25
	Such comfort as do lusty young men feel
	When well-apparelled April on the heel
	Of limping winter treads – even such delight
	Among fresh female buds shall you this night
	Inherit at my house. Hear all, all see, 30
	And like her most whose merit most shall be –
	Which on more view of many, mine, being one,
	May stand in number, though in reckoning none.

Capulet gives his servant a list of the guests to be invited to the feast. The servant cannot read and so asks Romeo and Benvolio for help.

34 **sirrah**: you there

37 **stay**: wait

39 **meddle**: busy himself
    yard: measuring rod
40 **last**: wooden foot shape used by shoemakers

47 **another's anguish**: the suffering of a second pain
48 **holp**: helped
    backward: in reverse
49 **another's languish**: a further suffering
51 **rank**: foul
52 **plantain leaf**: leaf used to help cuts heal

53 **broken shin**: cut on the leg

55 **bound**: tied up

57 **Good e'en**: i.e. Good afternoon

58 **gi'**: give you

60 **without book**: 1 by heart; 2 from experience

Think about

- In productions, this servant is usually Peter (the Nurse's man in Act 2 Scene 4) and would have been played by the comic actor in Shakespeare's company. If you were the director, what would you want the actor playing him to do in order to make this scene funny?

- What does Benvolio think about Romeo's behaviour?

Come, go with me.
(*To the* SERVANT, *giving him a guest-list*)
                    Go, sirrah, trudge about
Through fair Verona. Find those persons out   35
Whose names are written there, and to them say
My house and welcome on their pleasure stay.

Exit CAPULET, *with* PARIS.

SERVANT   Find them out whose names are written here? It is
            written that the shoemaker should meddle with his yard
            and the tailor with his last, the fisher with his pencil and   40
            the painter with his nets. But I am sent to find those
            persons whose names are here writ, and can never find
            what names the writing person hath here writ. I must to
            the learnèd. (*He sees* BENVOLIO *and* ROMEO *coming*) In
            good time!   45

Enter BENVOLIO *and* ROMEO.

BENVOLIO   Tut, man, one fire burns out another's burning!
            One pain is lessened by another's anguish:
            Turn giddy, and be holp by backward turning.
            One desperate grief cures with another's languish:
            Take thou some new infection to thy eye,   50
            And the rank poison of the old will die.

ROMEO   Your plantain leaf is excellent for that.

BENVOLIO   For what, I pray thee?

ROMEO   For your broken shin.

BENVOLIO   Why, Romeo, art thou mad?

ROMEO   Not mad, but bound more than a madman is –   55
            Shut up in prison, kept without my food,
            Whipped and tormented, and – Good e'en, good fellow.

SERVANT   God gi' good e'en. I pray, sir, can you read?

ROMEO   Ay – mine own fortune in my misery.

SERVANT   Perhaps you have learned it without book. But I pray,   60
            can you read anything you see?

ROMEO   Ay, if I know the letters and the language.

Romeo reads out the guest-list, which includes the girl he loves – Rosaline. Benvolio suggests that they should go to the feast, where Romeo can see other girls who are more beautiful.

63 Rest you merry: i.e. Goodbye and good luck

66 County: Count

83 crush: drink

86 Sups: has supper

88 unattainted: unbiased

Think about

- Look at lines 46 to 51, and 85 to 90. What advice does Benvolio give Romeo?

92 Maintains such falsehood: accepts lies like that
93 these: i.e. my eyes

SERVANT	Ye say honestly. (*Walking away*) Rest you merry.
ROMEO	Stay, fellow! I can read. (*He takes the guest-list and reads it*)

'Signior Martino and his wife and daughters;   65
County Anselme and his beauteous sisters;
The lady widow of Vitruvio;
Signior Placentio and his lovely nieces;
Mercutio and his brother Valentine;
Mine uncle Capulet, his wife and daughters;   70
My fair niece Rosaline and Livia;
Signior Valentio and his cousin Tybalt;
Lucio and the lively Helena.'
A fair assembly! Whither should they come?

SERVANT	Up – 75
ROMEO	Whither? To supper?
SERVANT	To our house.
ROMEO	Whose house?
SERVANT	My master's.
ROMEO	Indeed, I should have asked thee that before. 80
SERVANT	Now I'll tell you without asking. My master is the great rich Capulet – and if you be not of the house of Montagues, I pray come and crush a cup of wine. Rest you merry.

Exit.

BENVOLIO	At this same ancient feast of Capulet's 85

Sups the fair Rosaline whom thou so loves,
With all the admirèd beauties of Verona.
Go thither, and with unattainted eye
Compare her face with some that I shall show,
And I will make thee think thy swan a crow.   90

ROMEO	When the devout religion of mine eye

Maintains such falsehood, then turn tears to fire;
And these who, often drowned, could never die,

43

Romeo agrees to go to the Capulet feast, but refuses to accept that he will find any girl there more beautiful than Rosaline.

94 **Transparent**: 1 bright / clear; 2 obvious
heretics: disbelievers (in a religion), who might be executed by burning

97 **none ... by**: when there were no other beauties present

98 **poised**: only balanced

99 **that ... scales**: i.e. those eyes

102 **scant**: hardly

104 **splendour ... own**: i.e. Rosaline's beauty

Think about

• How does Romeo respond to Benvolio's advice?

• What do you notice about the language Romeo uses in describing his love in lines 91 to 94? Think about the meanings of 'devout' and 'heretics', for example. What point is he making?

	Transparent heretics, be burnt for liars.	
	One fairer than my love? The all-seeing sun	95
	Ne'er saw her match since first the world begun!	
BENVOLIO	Tut, you saw her fair, none else being by –	
	Herself poised with herself in either eye.	
	But in that crystal scales let there be weighed	
	Your lady's love against some other maid	100
	That I will show you shining at this feast,	
	And she shall scant show well that now seems best.	
ROMEO	I'll go along – no such sight to be shown,	
	But to rejoice in splendour of mine own.	

Exeunt.

In this scene ...

- Lady Capulet tells Juliet that Count Paris wants to marry her.
- Juliet agrees to consider Paris as a husband.

Lady Capulet and the Nurse discuss Juliet's age. The Nurse recalls an event from Juliet's childhood.

2 **maidenhead**: virginity
3 **God forbid**: Perhaps the Nurse has realised that 'lady-bird' was sometimes slang for prostitute.

8 **the matter**: what I want to talk about
   give leave: leave us alone
10 **thou's**: you shall
   counsel: private discussion
11 **pretty age**: i.e. the right age for marriage

14 **teen**: grief
15 **but**: only
16 **Lammas-tide**: a harvest feast on August 1st
17 **odd**: a few

19 **Susan**: the Nurse's own daughter (who died young)

24 **was weaned**: stopped being breast-fed
26 **laid ... dug**: Women would put the bitter-tasting substance on the nipple to put the child off sucking.
28 **bear a brain**: have a great memory

Think about

- Why does Lady Capulet call the Nurse back in line 9, do you think? Think about what the dialogue on this page reveals about the status of the Nurse in the Capulet household.

Inside the house of the Capulets.

Enter LADY CAPULET *and the* NURSE.

LADY CAPULET Nurse, where's my daughter? Call her forth to me.

NURSE Now, by my maidenhead at twelve year old, I bade her
come. What, lamb! What, lady-bird! God forbid!
Where's this girl? What, Juliet!

Enter JULIET.

JULIET How now? Who calls?   5

NURSE Your mother.

JULIET Madam, I am here. What is your will?

LADY CAPULET This is the matter. Nurse, give leave a while –
We must talk in secret. – Nurse, come back again.
I have remembered me, thou's hear our counsel.   10
Thou know'st my daughter's of a pretty age.

NURSE Faith, I can tell her age unto an hour.

LADY CAPULET She's not fourteen.

NURSE I'll lay fourteen of my teeth – and yet, to my teen
be it spoken, I have but four – she's not fourteen.   15
How long is it now to Lammas-tide?

LADY CAPULET A fortnight and odd days.

NURSE Even or odd, of all days in the year come Lammas-Eve
at night shall she be fourteen. Susan and she – God rest
all Christian souls – were of an age. Well, Susan is with   20
God: she was too good for me. But, as I said, on
Lammas-Eve at night shall she be fourteen – that shall
she, marry, I remember it well. 'Tis since the earthquake
now eleven years, and she was weaned – I never shall
forget it – of all the days of the year, upon that day. For 25
I had then laid wormwood to my dug, sitting in the sun
under the dove-house wall. My lord and you were then
at Mantua – nay, I do bear a brain! But, as I said, when

The Nurse finishes her story and Lady Capulet asks Juliet how she feels about marriage.

29 **dug**: breast

30 **tetchy**: irritable

31 **Shake ... dove-house**: the dove-house shook

32 **I trow**: believe me
    bid me trudge: tell me to go away

33 **stand high-lone**: stand up by herself

33–4 **by the rood**: by the holy cross (an oath)

35 **broke her brow**: cut her forehead

36 **'a**: he

38 **fall backward**: a sexual double-meaning

38–9 **hast more wit**: know a bit more

39 **by my holidame**: by my holiness (an oath)

41 **come about**: come true eventually
    warrant: promise you
    and I should: even if I were to

43 **stinted**: stopped

47 **it**: its

48 **stone**: testicle

50 **comest to age**: are old enough

54 **And I might**: If only I could

55 **once**: one day

56 **Marry**: by (the Virgin) Mary

58 **How ... married**: What do you think of the idea of getting married

61 **thy teat**: the nipple you sucked (i.e. the Nurse's)

Think about

• What are your first impressions of the Nurse?

• If you were the director, how would you ask the actor playing Lady Capulet to react while the Nurse is telling – and repeating – her story (lines 18 to 55)?

it did taste the wormwood on the nipple of my dug and
felt it bitter, pretty fool, to see it tetchy, and fall out with   30
the dug! 'Shake', quoth the dove-house. 'Twas no need,
I trow, to bid me trudge. And since that time it is eleven
years for then she could stand high-lone. Nay, by the
rood, she could have run and waddled all about – for
even the day before, she broke her brow, and then my   35
husband – God be with his soul, 'a was a merry man –
took up the child. 'Yea,' quoth he, 'dost thou fall upon
thy face? Thou wilt fall backward when thou hast more
wit, wilt thou not, Jule?' And, by my holidame, the pretty
wretch left crying, and said 'Ay'. To see now how a jest   40
shall come about! I warrant, and I should live a thousand
years, I never should forget it. 'Wilt thou not, Jule?' quoth
he – and, pretty fool, it stinted, and said 'Ay'!

LADY CAPULET   Enough of this. I pray thee hold thy peace.

NURSE   Yes, madam. Yet I cannot choose but laugh, to think it   45
should leave crying, and say 'Ay'. And yet I warrant it
had upon it brow a bump as big as a young cockerel's
stone – a perilous knock! – and it cried bitterly. 'Yea,'
quoth my husband, 'fall'st upon thy face? Thou wilt fall
backward when thou comest to age, wilt thou not, Jule?'   50
It stinted, and said 'Ay'!

JULIET   And stint thou too, I pray thee, Nurse, say I.

NURSE   Peace, I have done. God mark thee to his grace, thou
wast the prettiest babe that e'er I nursed. And I might
live to see thee married once, I have my wish.   55

LADY CAPULET   Marry, that 'marry' is the very theme
I came to talk of. Tell me, daughter Juliet,
How stands your dispositions to be married?

JULIET   It is an honour that I dream not of.

NURSE   An honour! Were not I thine only nurse, I would say   60
thou hadst sucked wisdom from thy teat.

Juliet is told that Paris wants to marry her. She cautiously agrees to consider him as a husband.

63 **ladies of esteem**: honourable society women

65 **much ... years**: at roughly the same age

69 **a man of wax**: i.e. the ideal model of a man

76 **every married lineament**: all his features, combined in harmony

77 **one ... content**: each one goes well with another

78 **what obscured**: whatever you cannot see clearly

79 **margent**: margin (which often contained notes and comments)

80 **unbound**: 1 without a cover; 2 unmarried

81 **cover**: i.e. a wife

82 **lives in the sea**: i.e. knows where it is supposed to live

82–3 **'tis much ... hide**: the cover of a book should reflect the beautiful contents (i.e. Juliet would show off Paris's worth)

84–5 **That book ... story**: i.e. people admire a book both for its fine story and its rich binding

86–7 **share ... less**: i.e. be admired as much as Paris is when you are married to him

88 **grow**: 1 gain in status; 2 become pregnant

90 **I'll look ... move**: I expect I shall like him, if I am attracted by his looks

91–2 **no more ... fly**: I will go no further in love except with your permission

95 **in extremity**: in a mess

96 **wait**: serve at table
straight: immediately

Think about

• What do Lady Capulet's speeches, in lines 62 to 67, and 72 to 87, reveal about her attitude to love and marriage?

LADY CAPULET   Well, think of marriage now. Younger than you,
Here in Verona, ladies of esteem,
Are made already mothers. By my count,
I was your mother much upon these years   65
That you are now a maid. Thus then in brief:
The valiant Paris seeks you for his love.

NURSE   A man, young lady! Lady, such a man as all the world
... Why, he's a man of wax!

LADY CAPULET   Verona's summer hath not such a flower.   70

NURSE   Nay, he's a flower – in faith, a very flower!

LADY CAPULET   What say you? Can you love the gentleman?
This night you shall behold him at our feast.
Read o'er the volume of young Paris' face,
And find delight writ there with beauty's pen.   75
Examine every married lineament,
And see how one another lends content –
And what obscured in this fair volume lies,
Find written in the margent of his eyes.
This precious book of love, this unbound lover,   80
To beautify him, only lacks a cover.
The fish lives in the sea – and 'tis much pride
For fair without the fair within to hide.
That book in many's eyes doth share the glory
That in gold clasps locks in the golden story.   85
So shall you share all that he doth possess
By having him, making yourself no less.

NURSE   No less? Nay, bigger! Women grow by men.

LADY CAPULET   Speak briefly: can you like of Paris' love?

JULIET   I'll look to like, if looking liking move.   90
But no more deep will I endart mine eye
Than your consent gives strength to make it fly.

Enter the SERVANT.

SERVANT   Madam, the guests are come, supper served up, you
called, my young lady asked for, the Nurse cursed in the
pantry, and everything in extremity. I must hence to 95
wait. I beseech you, follow straight.

They go off to the feast where
Paris is waiting to meet Juliet.

97 **the County stays**: Count Paris is
waiting
98 **to**: to add to

---**Think about**---

- What kind of relationship to
  Juliet does the Nurse have?
  How can you tell?

- What does this scene reveal
  about the relationship
  between Lady Capulet and
  Juliet? Think about how
  close they are, for example.

LADY CAPULET We follow thee. Juliet, the County stays.

NURSE Go, girl. Seek happy nights to happy days.

Exeunt.

ACT 1 SCENE 4

In this scene ...

- Romeo has had a dream which has made him uneasy about attending the Capulet feast.
- Mercutio tells him about Queen Mab and declares that dreams are only trivial fantasies.
- They enter the Capulet house, despite Romeo's concerns.

Romeo, Benvolio and their friend Mercutio arrive outside the Capulets' house. Mercutio tries to shake Romeo out of his love-sickness.

Think about

- What effects has love had on Romeo, according to his statements here?

- Why do you think Mercutio might have an invitation to the Capulets' feast, while the others don't? Look back at Act 1 Scene 2, line 69.

1 **speech ... excuse**: Maskers would introduce themselves with an introductory speech.

3 **The date ... prolixity**: i.e. These days such long-winded speeches are unfashionable

4 **hoodwinked**: blindfolded

5 **Tartar's ... lath**: typical Cupid's bow, made of cheap wood (i.e. a prop)

6 **crow-keeper**: scarecrow

7 **without-book**: learned by heart

8 **After the prompter**: with the prompter's help

10 **measure ... measure**: 'serve them' a dance

11 **ambling**: dancing

12 **heavy**: low-spirited

16 **stakes**: fixes

18 **above ... bound**: higher than an ordinary leap in dancing

19 **sore ... shaft**: seriously wounded by Cupid's arrow

21 **bound a pitch**: i.e. leap up high

23 **sink in it**: enjoy love-making

24 **oppression**: weight
    tender thing: delicate female

26 **rude**: rough

Outside the house of the Capulets.

Enter Romeo, Benvolio, *and* Mercutio, *with five or six other gentlemen wearing masks. Servants light their way with flaming torches, and one carries a drum.*

Romeo	What, shall this speech be spoke for our excuse?
	Or shall we on without apology?
Benvolio	The date is out of such prolixity.
	We'll have no Cupid hoodwinked with a scarf,
	Bearing a Tartar's painted bow of lath, 5
	Scaring the ladies like a crow-keeper –
	Nor no without-book prologue, faintly spoke
	After the prompter, for our entrance.
	But let them measure us by what they will,
	We'll measure them a measure and be gone. 10
Romeo	Give me a torch: I am not for this ambling.
	Being but heavy, I will bear the light.
Mercutio	Nay, gentle Romeo, we must have you dance.
Romeo	Not I, believe me. You have dancing shoes
	With nimble soles: I have a soul of lead 15
	So stakes me to the ground I cannot move.
Mercutio	You are a lover: borrow Cupid's wings,
	And soar with them above a common bound.
Romeo	I am too sore empiercèd with his shaft
	To soar with his light feathers – and so bound, 20
	I cannot bound a pitch above dull woe.
	Under love's heavy burden do I sink.
Mercutio	And to sink in it should you burden love –
	Too great oppression for a tender thing.
Romeo	Is love a tender thing? It is too rough, 25
	Too rude, too boisterous, and it pricks like thorn.

Romeo has worries about attending the feast because he has had a disturbing dream. Mercutio tells him that he must have been visited by Queen Mab.

28 **Prick ... pricking**: 1 hurt love in return for hurting you; 2 ease sexual desire by satisfying it
29 **case**: cover (mask)
   visage: face
30 **visor for a visor**: mask for an ugly face
31 **What ... deformities**: if nosy people notice my ugliness
32 **beetle ... me**: i.e. the mask has overhanging eyebrows and red cheeks
34 **betake ... legs**: start dancing
35 **wantons**: irresponsible people
37-8 **proverbed ... on**: the old proverb applies to me: 'the onlooker sees the best of the game'
39 **The game ... done**: i.e. Let's quit while we are ahead
40 **dun's the mouse**: 'be silent and unseen' (a proverb)
41 **Dun**: a stick-in-the-mud
   draw ... mire: pull you out of the mud
42 **save your reverence**: if you'll excuse me for saying so
43 **burn daylight**: waste time
46 **good**: intended
46-7 **our judgement ... wits**: there is five times more sense in that than in what our senses usually tell us
49 **no wit**: not wise

Think about

• Mercutio and Romeo love playing with words. Look at the puns in lines 9 to 10, 12, 15, 18 to 19, 20 to 21, 26 to 28, 30, 39 to 41, and 51. Do you find them irritating or entertaining?

56

MERCUTIO	If love be rough with you, be rough with love:
	Prick love for pricking, and you beat love down.
	Give me a case to put my visage in:
	A visor for a visor! What care I	30
	What curious eye doth quote deformities?
	Here are the beetle brows shall blush for me.

He puts on a mask.

| BENVOLIO | Come, knock and enter – and no sooner in, |
| | But every man betake him to his legs. |

ROMEO	A torch for me. Let wantons light of heart	35
	Tickle the senseless rushes with their heels,
	For I am proverbed with a grandsire phrase:
	I'll be a candle-holder and look on.
	The game was ne'er so fair, and I am done.

MERCUTIO	Tut, dun's the mouse, the constable's own word.	40
	If thou art Dun, we'll draw thee from the mire –
	Or, save your reverence, love, wherein thou stickest
	Up to the ears. Come, we burn daylight, ho!

| ROMEO | Nay, that's not so. |

MERCUTIO	I mean, sir, in delay
	We waste our lights in vain, like lights by day.	45
	Take our good meaning, for our judgement sits
	Five times in that, ere once in our five wits.

| ROMEO | And we mean well in going to this mask – |
| | But 'tis no wit to go. |

| MERCUTIO | Why, may one ask? |

| ROMEO | I dreamt a dream tonight. |

| MERCUTIO | And so did I. | 50 |

| ROMEO | Well, what was yours? |

| MERCUTIO | That dreamers often lie. |

| ROMEO | In bed asleep, while they do dream things true. |

| MERCUTIO | O, then I see Queen Mab hath been with you. |

| BENVOLIO | Queen Mab? What's she? |

Mercutio tells them who Queen Mab is and what she does while people are asleep.

55 **midwife**: i.e. she 'delivers' people's dreams

57 **On ... alderman**: on the ring of a senior town councillor

58 **atomies**: tiny creatures

60 **spinners**: spiders

61 **cover**: canopy

62 **traces**: harness

64 **film**: gossamer

66–7 **worm ... maid**: It was believed that worms grew in lazy girls' fingers.

69 **joiner-squirrel**: The squirrel hollows out nuts like a carpenter.

70 **Time ... mind**: for as long as people can remember

71 **state**: splendour

73 **on curtsies**: of bowing (and flattering people)
straight: immediately

79 **smelling ... suit**: finding a client who will pay to have their case argued at court

80 **tithe-pig**: Pigs were sometimes given as the tenth of a person's income which had to go to the parson.

82 **benefice**: paid church appointment

85 **breaches**: attacks through gaps blown in castle walls
ambuscadoes: ambushes

86 **healths ... deep**: i.e. heavy drinking
anon: immediately

90 **plaits**: tangles

91 **bakes ... hairs**: makes unclean people's hair matted

92 **much misfortune bodes**: is very unlucky

93 **hag**: evil fairy

Think about

• How could the actor playing Mercutio make the very long Queen Mab speech (lines 55 to 96) come alive for the audience? Think about what actions might accompany it, for example.

| MERCUTIO | She is the fairies' midwife – and she comes | 55 |

MERCUTIO   She is the fairies' midwife – and she comes   55
           In shape no bigger than an agate stone
           On the forefinger of an alderman,
           Drawn with a team of little atomies
           Over men's noses as they lie asleep.
           Her waggon-spokes made of long spinners' legs,   60
           The cover of the wings of grasshoppers,
           Her traces of the smallest spider-web,
           Her collars of the moonshine's watery beams,
           Her whip of cricket's bone, the lash of film –
           Her waggoner a small grey-coated gnat,   65
           Not half so big as a round little worm
           Pricked from the lazy finger of a maid.
           Her chariot is an empty hazel-nut,
           Made by the joiner-squirrel or old grub,
           Time out o' mind the fairies' coachmakers.   70
           And in this state she gallops night by night
           Through lovers' brains, and then they dream of love;
           O'er courtiers' knees, that dream on curtsies straight;
           O'er lawyers' fingers, who straight dream on fees;
           O'er ladies' lips, who straight on kisses dream –   75
           Which oft the angry Mab with blisters plagues,
           Because their breaths with sweetmeats tainted are.
           Sometime she gallops o'er a courtier's nose
           And then dreams he of smelling out a suit;
           And sometime comes she with a tithe-pig's tail,   80
           Tickling a parson's nose as 'a lies asleep:
           Then dreams he of another benefice.
           Sometime she driveth o'er a soldier's neck,
           And then dreams he of cutting foreign throats,
           Of breaches, ambuscadoes, Spanish blades,   85
           Of healths five fathom deep – and then anon
           Drums in his ear, at which he starts and wakes,
           And being thus frighted, swears a prayer or two,
           And sleeps again. This is that very Mab
           That plaits the manes of horses in the night,   90
           And bakes the elf-locks in foul sluttish hairs,
           Which, once untangled, much misfortune bodes.
           This is the hag, when maids lie on their backs,

Mercutio claims that dreams are nothing more than trivial fantasies. They go in to the feast, despite Romeo's uneasiness that the evening may lead to future tragedy.

94 **learns**: teaches
bear: 1 bear the weight of a man; 2 bear children

95 **of good carriage**: 1 graceful; 2 good at love-making

97 **nothing**: could mean 'no-thing' (the female sexual organ)

99 **Begot**: born
vain fantasy: idle dreaming

104 **Turning his side**: reversing his direction

105 **blows ... ourselves**: distracts us from our intentions

107 **my mind misgives**: I have an uneasy feeling

108 **yet ... stars**: fated to happen, but not yet revealed

109 **date**: appointed time

110–11 **expire ... Of**: put an end to

112 **vile forfeit**: awful penalty
untimely: early

113 **He**: God
steerage of my course: control over my direction

---Think about---

• In some productions, Mercutio has to be stopped by Romeo (line 96) because he seems to be building up into a mad frenzy. What do you think the Queen Mab speech reveals about him?

• What seems to be worrying Romeo as they approach the party? Do you think that he is just in low spirits, or does he have some genuine sense of the fate in store for him?

	That presses them and learns them first to bear,	
	Making them women of good carriage.	95
	This is she –	

ROMEO   Peace, peace, Mercutio, peace!
Thou talk'st of nothing.

MERCUTIO   True, I talk of dreams,
Which are the children of an idle brain,
Begot of nothing but vain fantasy,
Which is as thin of substance as the air,   100
And more inconstant than the wind, who woos
Even now the frozen bosom of the north,
And being angered, puffs away from thence,
Turning his side to the dew-dropping south.

BENVOLIO   This wind you talk of blows us from ourselves: 105
Supper is done, and we shall come too late.

ROMEO   I fear, too early – for my mind misgives
Some consequence, yet hanging in the stars,
Shall bitterly begin his fearful date
With this night's revels, and expire the term   110
Of a despisèd life closed in my breast,
By some vile forfeit of untimely death.
But He that hath the steerage of my course
Direct my sail! On, lusty gentlemen.

BENVOLIO   Strike, drum!   115

ROMEO *and* BENVOLIO *put on their masks. All the maskers
march round to the beat of the drum, then exeunt.*

In this scene ...

- Tybalt is bitterly angry that Romeo has gate-crashed the Capulet feast, and says that he will not forget the insult.
- Romeo meets Juliet and they quickly begin to fall in love.
- After the lovers part, each is shocked to find out that they have fallen in love with someone who should be their enemy.

The household servants clear away after the feast and prepare the room for dancing. Capulet warmly welcomes his guests.

1 **take away**: remove the dirty dishes
2 **trencher**: plate

5 **joint-stools**: seats (stools made by joiners)
5–6 **court-cupboard**: sideboard
6 **look to the plate**: deal with the silverware
   Good thou: Be a good man
7 **march-pane**: marzipan
8 **Susan … Nell**: probably the servant's girl-friends

14 **longer … all**: survivor takes all
s.d. **maskers**: masked guests

Think about

- How would you direct the opening of this scene to make it energetic and full of life?

- What aspect of Capulet's personality that we have not seen before is revealed by his behaviour in lines 15 to 40?

16 **walk a bout**: have a dance

18 **deny**: refuse
   makes dainty: seems reluctant
19 **Am I come near**: Have I guessed the truth

The great hall in the Capulets' house.

Enter two household SERVANTS, *clearing away after the feast.*

Enter ROMEO, MERCUTIO, BENVOLIO, *and their company, all in*
masks. They stand to one side as the SERVANTS *begin to clear*
the hall for dancing.

SERVANT 1	Where's Potpan, that he helps not to take away? He shift a trencher? He scrape a trencher?
SERVANT 2	When good manners shall lie all in one or two men's hands, and they unwashed too, 'tis a foul thing.
SERVANT 1	Away with the joint-stools, remove the court-cupboard, look to the plate. Good thou, save me a piece of march-pane – and, as thou loves me, let the porter let in Susan Grindstone and Nell. (*He calls*) Antony and Potpan!

Enter two more SERVANTS.

SERVANT 3	Ay, boy, ready.
SERVANT 1	You are looked for and called for, asked for and sought for, in the great chamber.
SERVANT 4	We cannot be here and there too. Cheerly, boys! Be brisk a while, and the longer liver take all.

Enter CAPULET *and* LADY CAPULET, *Capulets' older* COUSIN,
JULIET, *the* NURSE, *and* TYBALT, *with his page-boy. The other*
guests from the feast, and musicians, follow.

The SERVANTS *stand aside.* CAPULET *greets the maskers.*

CAPULET	Welcome, gentlemen! Ladies that have their toes Unplagued with corns will walk a bout with you. Ah ha, my mistresses! Which of you all Will now deny to dance? She that makes dainty, She, I'll swear, hath corns. Am I come near ye now? Welcome, gentlemen. I have seen the day

5

10

15

20

Capulet and his cousin talk fondly about their younger days. As the guests dance, Romeo sets eyes on Juliet and is stunned by her beauty.

21 **visor**: mask

25 **A hall**: Make some space
foot it: get dancing
26 **turn ... up**: pack away the trestle tables
28 **unlooked-for sport**: unexpected entertainment

32 **By 'r lady:** By the Virgin Mary (an oath)

34 **nuptial**: wedding
35 **Pentecost**: Whitsun

39 **a ward**: i.e. he had a guardian as he was not of age

Think about

• What words and phrases reveal that Romeo is thinking of Juliet's beauty in terms of brightness in contrast to the surrounding dark? Look at lines 44 to 53.

46 **Ethiop**: in Shakespeare's time, any black African
47 **dear**: precious

> That I have worn a visor, and could tell
> A whispering tale in a fair lady's ear
> Such as would please. – 'Tis gone, 'tis gone, 'tis gone!
> You are welcome, gentlemen! Come, musicians, play!

The maskers mingle with the other guests. Music, and a dance, begins.

> A hall, a hall – give room! And foot it, girls!   **25**
> (*To the* SERVANTS) More light, you knaves, and turn the
>   tables up! –
> And quench the fire, the room is grown too hot.
> – Ah, sirrah, this unlooked-for sport comes well!
> Nay sit, nay sit, good Cousin Capulet –
> For you and I are past our dancing days.   **30**
> How long is't now since last yourself and I
> Were in a mask?

COUSIN   By 'r lady, thirty years.

CAPULET   What, man? 'Tis not so much, 'tis not so much!
                 'Tis since the nuptial of Lucentio –
                 Come Pentecost as quickly as it will –   **35**
                 Some five and twenty years, and then we masked.

COUSIN   'Tis more, 'tis more. His son is elder, sir:
                 His son is thirty.

CAPULET   Will you tell me that?
                 His son was but a ward two years ago.
                 (*Watching the dance*) Good youth i' faith. O, youth's
                     a jolly thing!   **40**

ROMEO   (*To a* SERVANT) What lady's that which doth enrich the
                     hand
                 Of yonder knight?

SERVANT   I know not, sir.

ROMEO   O, she doth teach the torches to burn bright!
                 It seems she hangs upon the cheek of night   **45**
                 As a rich jewel in an Ethiop's ear –
                 Beauty too rich for use, for earth too dear.
                 So shows a snowy dove trooping with crows,
                 As yonder lady o'er her fellows shows.

Tybalt recognises Romeo and angrily reports his discovery of the gate-crasher to Capulet. Capulet has heard good things about Romeo and loses his temper with Tybalt for threatening to disturb the party.

50 **The measure done**: Once this dance is over
51 **rude**: rough (compared with Juliet's)
52 **Forswear it**: Swear that it was not so

55 **rapier**: sword

55 **slave**: villain
56 **antic face**: comic, grotesque mask
57 **fleer ... solemnity**: mock our celebrations
58 **stock ... kin**: my family honour
59 **hold**: consider
60 **storm**: behave so angrily

62 **spite**: contempt

Think about

• What does Romeo's language tell you about the nature of his feelings for Juliet at first sight, for example in line 52?

• If you were the director, how would you ask Capulet and Tybalt to act during their confrontation (lines 54 to 92)? Think about how each character is feeling as the argument becomes heated, how they should say particular lines, and what actions they might perform.

65 **Content thee**: Calm down
66 **'A bears him**: He behaves
   portly: well-mannered
68 **well-governed**: good-mannered

70 **do him disparagement**: treat him in an ill-mannered way

73 **Show ... presence**: behave pleasantly
74 **ill-beseeming semblance**: very inappropriate way to look

77 **goodman**: i.e. not a gentleman
   Go to: Stop this behaviour

80 **make a mutiny**: cause a disturbance
81 **set cock-a-hoop**: behave wildly

	The measure done, I'll watch her place of stand,	**50**
	And, touching hers, make blessèd my rude hand.	
	Did my heart love till now? Forswear it, sight! –	
	For I ne'er saw true beauty till this night.	

TYBALT	This, by his voice, should be a Montague.
	Fetch me my rapier, boy.

Exit PAGE.

	What! – Dares the slave	**55**
	Come hither, covered with an antic face,	
	To fleer and scorn at our solemnity?	
	Now, by the stock and honour of my kin,	
	To strike him dead I hold it not a sin!	

CAPULET	Why, how now, kinsman! Wherefore storm you so?	**60**

TYBALT	Uncle, this is a Montague, our foe! –
	A villain that is hither come in spite,
	To scorn at our solemnity this night.

CAPULET	Young Romeo is it?

TYBALT	'Tis he, that villain Romeo.

CAPULET	Content thee, gentle coz, let him alone.	**65**
	'A bears him like a portly gentleman –	
	And to say truth, Verona brags of him	
	To be a virtuous and well-governed youth.	
	I would not, for the wealth of all this town,	
	Here in my house do him disparagement.	**70**
	Therefore be patient, take no note of him.	
	It is my will, the which if thou respect,	
	Show a fair presence and put off these frowns,	
	An ill-beseeming semblance for a feast.	

TYBALT	It fits when such a villain is a guest.	**75**
	I'll not endure him!	

CAPULET	He shall be endured.
	What, goodman boy? I say he shall! Go to!
	Am I the master here, or you? Go to!
	You'll not endure him! God shall mend my soul,
	You'll make a mutiny among my guests!
	You will set cock-a-hoop! You'll be the man!

(Line numbers: 80 at "You'll make a mutiny among my guests!")

Tybalt backs down from confronting Romeo, but plans revenge. Romeo and Juliet meet and exchange loving words.

82 **shame**: insult

83 **saucy**: insolent
84 **trick ... scathe you**: stupid behaviour might do you harm
85 **contrary *me***: go against *my* will
86 **Well said**: Bravo
    princox: young upstart

89 **perforce**: forced upon me
    wilful choler: the anger I want to show
90 **in ... greeting**: i.e. they are in conflict
92 **gall**: poison

Think about

• What impression have you formed of Tybalt from this scene and Act 1 Scene 1?

• Lines 93 to 106 are written in the form of a sonnet. (This was a fourteen-line poem, divided into sections, often used by poets writing about love-affairs.) How are the different stages in the dialogue between Romeo and Juliet represented through the three sections (93 to 96, 97 to 100, and 101 to 106)?

---

93 **profane**: debase / make dirty
94 **holy shrine**: i.e. Juliet's hand
95 **pilgrims**: people who travel to holy places

97 **you do wrong**: i.e. your hand was not rough – so no kiss was called for
98 **mannerly**: proper / fitting
100 **palm to ... kiss**: Pilgrims would touch a holy statue's hand, not kiss it. (Pilgrims also carried palm-leaves.)

105 **Saints ... move**: 1 Statues do not move; 2 Saints do not set things in motion
    grant ... sake: they answer prayers

TYBALT	Why, uncle, 'tis a shame.

CAPULET	Go to, go to!

You are a saucy boy! Is't so indeed?
This trick may chance to scathe you. – I know what.
You must contrary *me*! Marry, 'tis time –   85
(*To dancers nearby*) Well said, my hearts! – You are a
     princox! Go!
Be quiet, or – (*To the* SERVANTS) More light, more light,
     for shame! –
I'll make you quiet! – (*To dancers*) What! – Cheerly
     my hearts!

He leaves TYBALT, *and goes back to his guests as the dancing continues.*

TYBALT	Patience perforce with wilful choler meeting

Makes my flesh tremble in their different greeting.   90
I will withdraw. But this intrusion shall,
Now seeming sweet, convert to bitterest gall!

                                                                                    Exit.

ROMEO	(*Taking* JULIET's *hand*) If I profane with my unworthiest

     hand
This holy shrine, the gentle sin is this:
My lips, two blushing pilgrims, ready stand   95
To smooth that rough touch with a tender kiss.

JULIET	Good pilgrim, you do wrong your hand too much,

Which mannerly devotion shows in this –
For saints have hands that pilgrims' hands do touch,
And palm to palm is holy palmers' kiss.   100

ROMEO	Have not saints lips, and holy palmers too?

JULIET	Ay, pilgrim, lips that they must use in prayer.

ROMEO	O then, dear saint, let lips do what hands do:

They pray: grant thou – lest faith turn to despair.

JULIET	Saints do not move, though grant for prayers' sake. 105

Romeo and Juliet kiss. The
Nurse interrupts, telling Juliet
that her mother wants her.
Romeo asks the Nurse who
Juliet is and is dismayed to hear
that she is a Capulet. He and his
friends leave.

106 move not: remain still

107 purged: purified

109 trespass ... urged: you encouraged this
sin very sweetly

110 by the book: like an expert

112 What: Who

115 withal: with

117 the chinks: plenty of money

118 O dear account: What a heavy price
to pay
my foe's debt: i.e. in the power of my
enemy
119 The ... best: Let's quit while we're
ahead
122 trifling ... towards: there are light
refreshments on the way

126 fay: faith
it waxes: it's getting

Think about

• How seriously should we
take Romeo's new-found
love for Juliet? Does his
language suggest that he is
now genuinely in love, or is
this just another infatuation?

• What does the religious
imagery used by Romeo
and Juliet suggest about the
way they view their love?
How does it affect the way
we see it?

ROMEO   Then move not, while my prayer's effect I take.

He kisses her.

             Thus from my lips, by thine, my sin is purged.

JULIET   Then have my lips the sin that they have took.

ROMEO   Sin from my lips? O trespass sweetly urged!
             Give me my sin again.

He kisses her again.

JULIET   You kiss by the book.   110

NURSE   (*Approaching them*) Madam, your mother craves a
                 word with you.

ROMEO   (*As* JULIET *goes*) What is her mother?

NURSE   Marry, bachelor,
             Her mother is the lady of the house,
             And a good lady, and a wise and virtuous.
             I nursed her daughter that you talked withal.   115
             I tell you, he that can lay hold of her
             Shall have the chinks.

ROMEO   Is she a Capulet?
             O dear account! My life is my foe's debt.

BENVOLIO   Away, be gone! The sport is at the best.

ROMEO   Ay, so I fear – the more is my unrest.   120

CAPULET   Nay, gentleman, prepare not to be gone! –
             We have a trifling foolish banquet towards.

The maskers whisper their excuses to him.

             Is it e'en so? Why, then I thank you all.
             I thank you, honest gentlemen. Good night.
             (*To the* SERVANTS) More torches here! Come on, then
                 let's to bed.   125
             Ah, sirrah, by my fay, it waxes late –
             I'll to my rest.

*Torch-bearers show the maskers out. Guests prepare to
    depart. All exit, leaving only* JULIET *and the* NURSE.

When the Nurse tells Juliet who Romeo is, she realises that she has fallen in love with a Montague, the family she is supposed to hate.

128   **yond**: over there

135   **My grave ... bed**: I am likely to die unmarried

138   **sprung from**: born from
139   **Too ... late**: I saw him before I knew who he was; now that I know, it's too late
140   **Prodigious ... me**: This is a very ominous start to our love

143   **Anon**: Coming

Think about

- What have you learned about Juliet from this scene? Think about the differences between her attitudes to love and Romeo's attitudes, for example.

- Juliet finds a crafty way to find who the boy she has just met is (lines 128 to 134). What does she do? Why doesn't she just ask the Nurse outright?

JULIET	Come hither, Nurse. What is yond gentleman?
NURSE	The son and heir of old Tiberio.
JULIET	What's he that now is going out of door?

130

NURSE	Marry, that I think be young Petruchio.
JULIET	What's he that follows there, that would not dance?
NURSE	I know not.
JULIET	Go ask his name. (*Exit* NURSE) If he be marrièd, My grave is like to be my wedding bed.

135

NURSE	(***Returning***) His name is Romeo, and a Montague, The only son of your great enemy.
JULIET	My only love sprung from my only hate! Too early seen unknown, and known too late! Prodigious birth of love it is to me, That I must love a loathèd enemy.

140

NURSE	What's this? What's this?
JULIET	A rhyme I learnt even now Of one I danced withal.

JULIET *is called from another room.*

NURSE	Anon, anon! Come let's away. The strangers all are gone.

Exeunt.

Romeo and Juliet, 1996 (directed by B. Luhrmann)

Open Air Theatre, Regent's Park, 1986

Lyric Theatre, Hammersmith, 1995

Shakespeare's Globe, 2004

The Chorus talks about the change in Romeo's feelings and points out the obstacles in the way of Romeo and Juliet's love.

1 **old desire**: i.e. Romeo's old love for Rosaline
2 **young ... heir**: his new love longs to take its place
3 **fair**: beautiful woman
5 **again**: in return
6 **Alike**: both lovers equally
7 **foe supposed**: i.e. Juliet (a Capulet) **complain**: express his feelings / plead for love
10 **use to**: usually
11 **means**: opportunities

14 **Tempering ... sweet**: easing their difficult situation with the great sweetness of their meetings

Think about

• In some productions this second Chorus speech is cut. What purposes does it have? Would you cut it, or leave it in?

• A Shakespeare sonnet usually has three four-line sections (called 'quatrains') followed by a couplet. How does the sonnet form here help to express the situation that Romeo and Juliet are in?

Enter CHORUS.

CHORUS   Now old desire doth in his death-bed lie,
          And young affection gapes to be his heir.
          That fair for which love groaned for and would die,
          With tender Juliet matched, is now not fair.
          Now Romeo is beloved, and loves again,   5
          Alike bewitchèd by the charm of looks –
          But to his foe supposed he must complain,
          And she steal love's sweet bait from fearful hooks.
          Being held a foe, he may not have access
          To breathe such vows as lovers use to swear –   10
          And she as much in love, her means much less
          To meet her new-belovèd anywhere.
              But passion lends them power, time means, to meet,
              Tempering extremities with extreme sweet.

                                                        Exit.

In this scene ...

- Leaving the Capulet feast, Romeo hides from Benvolio and Mercutio.
- Mercutio speaks mockingly about Romeo's love for Rosaline and he and Benvolio leave.

Outside the Capulets' garden, Benvolio and Mercutio are looking for Romeo, who is listening, hidden. Mercutio pretends to be a magician trying to make Romeo appear.

2   **dull earth**: i.e. his physical body
    centre: heart, now in Juliet's possession

4   **stol'n him**: crept off secretly

5   **orchard**: garden

6   **conjure**: call him up, like a spirit
7   **Humours**: odd moods (i.e. 'moody')
8   **likeness**: form

10 **Ay me**: a lover's sigh
11 **gossip**: good old lady-friend
12 **purblind son and heir**: Cupid, her blind son
13 **Abraham**: i.e. rogue
    trim: accurately
14 **King Cophetua**: a king in an old ballad
16 **ape**: In fairgrounds apes were taught to lie 'dead' until 'revived' by a fake cure.

20 **demesnes**: estates (i.e. sexual parts)
    adjacent: nearby

Think about

- Mercutio talks about Cupid in line 13. Why do you think he is referred to so often in this play? Think about who he is, what his arrows represent, and why he is always shown blindfolded.

- How could the actor playing Mercutio do the 'conjuring' (lines 17 to 21)? What gestures and movements would make the scene comic?

The street, beside the gardens of the Capulet house.

Enter ROMEO, *walking away, then stopping.*

ROMEO	Can I go forward when my heart is here?
	Turn back, dull earth, and find thy centre out.

He scrambles into the garden and conceals himself as MERCUTIO *and* BENVOLIO *approach, and listens.*

Enter MERCUTIO *and* BENVOLIO.

BENVOLIO	Romeo! My cousin Romeo! Romeo!
MERCUTIO	He is wise,
	And on my life hath stol'n him home to bed.
BENVOLIO	He ran this way and leapt this orchard wall.
	Call, good Mercutio.
MERCUTIO	Nay, I'll conjure too.
	Romeo! Humours! Madman! Passion! Lover!
	Appear thou in the likeness of a sigh!
	Speak but one rhyme and I am satisfied –
	Cry but 'Ay me' – pronounce but 'love' and 'dove'! –
	Speak to my gossip Venus one fair word,
	One nickname for her purblind son and heir,
	Young Abraham Cupid – he that shot so trim
	When King Cophetua loved the beggar maid.
	He heareth not, he stirreth not, he moveth not! –
	The ape is dead, and I must conjure him.
	(*Imitating a magician trying to raise a spirit*)
	I conjure thee, by Rosaline's bright eyes,
	By her high forehead and her scarlet lip,
	By her fine foot, straight leg and quivering thigh,
	And the demesnes that there adjacent lie,
	That in thy likeness thou appear to us!
BENVOLIO	And if he hear thee, thou wilt anger him.

5

10

15

20

Mercutio makes sexual jokes about Romeo's love for Rosaline. He and Benvolio leave, believing that Romeo is hiding from them.

24 **raise**: can mean 'have an erection'
    spirit: can mean 'semen'
    circle: can mean 'vagina'
25 **stand**: be erect
26 **laid ... down**: had sex and satisfied him
27 **were some spite**: would really make him angry
    invocation: conjuring spell
31 **be consorted**: spend time
    humorous: 1 dark and humid; 2 moody
33 **mark**: target
34 **medlar**: kind of apple (thought to look like the female sexual organ)

37 **that**: if only
38 **open-arse**: another name for the medlar
    Poperin pear: kind of pear shaped like a penis (also wordplay on 'pop-her-in')
39 **truckle-bed**: i.e. my poor little bed
40 **field-bed**: i.e. sleeping in the open

42 **means**: intends

Think about

- Mercutio's language is full of sexual innuendoes (double-meanings), for example lines 24 to 29, and 38. What does that suggest about him and his attitude to women and love?

MERCUTIO	This cannot anger him. 'Twould anger him
	To raise a spirit in his mistress' circle,
	Of some strange nature, letting it there stand 25
	Till she had laid it, and conjured it down –
	That were some spite! My invocation
	Is fair and honest. In his mistress' name
	I conjure only but to raise up him.
BENVOLIO	Come. He hath hid himself among these trees 30
	To be consorted with the humorous night.
	Blind is his love, and best befits the dark.
MERCUTIO	If love be blind, love cannot hit the mark.
	Now will he sit under a medlar tree,
	And wish his mistress were that kind of fruit 35
	As maids call medlars when they laugh alone.
	O Romeo, that she were! O that she were
	An open-arse and thou a Poperin pear!
	Romeo, good night. I'll to my truckle-bed:
	This field-bed is too cold for me to sleep. 40
	Come, shall we go?
BENVOLIO	Go, then – for 'tis in vain
	To seek him here that means not to be found.

Exit, with MERCUTIO.

In this scene ...

- Inside the Capulets' garden, Romeo sees Juliet at her window.
- Not realising that Romeo is listening, Juliet speaks, and he answers her.
- Despite Juliet's worry that it is all happening so quickly, they declare their love for one another.
- Romeo promises to send Juliet a message the next morning explaining when and where they can be married, and they part.

Inside the Capulets' garden, Romeo sees Juliet at her bedroom window and marvels at her beauty. As he watches her, she speaks.

Think about

- What do the images Romeo uses suggest about the way he views Juliet? Look at lines 4 to 9, 15 to 22, and 26 to 32.

- What differences are there between Romeo's view of love and Mercutio's? Look, for example, at Act 1 Scene 4, lines 27 to 28, and Act 2 Scene 1.

2 **soft**: wait

6 **her maid**: As a virgin, Juliet is a 'hand-maid' of Diana, goddess of both the moon and chastity.

8 **vestal livery**: clothes worn by Diana's virgins
sick and green: Girls were thought to suffer from 'green-sickness', a thinness of the blood.

9 **fools**: Professional jesters also sometimes wore green as well as their traditional multi-coloured costume.

11 **O that**: I wish

13 **discourses**: speaks clearly

16 **entreat**: ask

17 **spheres**: People believed that planets and stars were fixed in crystal spheres encircling the earth.

18 **there**: i.e. in heaven

21 **airy region**: sky
stream: shine

28 **wingèd messenger**: angel

The garden, beside the Capulet house.

ROMEO *comes forward (reacting to* MERCUTIO's *joking).*

ROMEO He jests at scars that never felt a wound.

Enter JULIET, *coming to her window-balcony above.* ROMEO, *below, sees the light at the window, then realises it is* JULIET.

– But soft! What light through yonder window breaks?
It is the east, and Juliet is the sun.
Arise, fair sun, and kill the envious moon,
Who is already sick and pale with grief   5
That thou her maid art far more fair than she.
Be not her maid, since she is envious:
Her vestal livery is but sick and green,
And none but fools do wear it. Cast it off.
– It is my lady! – O, it is my love!   10
O that she knew she were!
She speaks – yet she says nothing. What of that?
Her eye discourses. I will answer it.
– I am too bold. 'Tis not to me she speaks.
Two of the fairest stars in all the heaven,   15
Having some business, do entreat her eyes
To twinkle in their spheres till they return.
What if her eyes were there, they in her head?
The brightness of her cheek would shame those stars
As daylight doth a lamp. Her eyes in heaven   20
Would through the airy region stream so bright
That birds would sing and think it were not night!
See how she leans her cheek upon her hand.
O that I were a glove upon that hand,
That I might touch that cheek!

JULIET   Ay me!

ROMEO   (*Aside*) She speaks.   25
O speak again, bright angel! – For thou art
As glorious to this night, being o'er my head,
As is a wingèd messenger of heaven

Not realising that he can hear her, Juliet declares that she loves Romeo despite the fact that he is a Montague. He calls out to her and she recognises his voice.

29 **white upturnèd**: looking up

31 **lazy-pacing**: slow-moving

33 **Wherefore art**: Why are

35 **be but**: only be

39 **though … Montague**: i.e. whatever you call yourself
40 **nor … nor**: neither … nor

46 **owes**: owns / possesses
47 **doff**: cast off
48 **for**: in exchange for

Think about

• What is Juliet saying about names in lines 38 to 49? What is she saying about the nature of enemies?

52 **bescreened in**: covered by the screen of
53 **counsel**: secret and private thoughts

• Is Juliet realistic in believing that names don't matter? Think about where names have been important and powerful earlier in the play: for example in the way the fight starts in Act 1 Scene 1, and for Juliet in Act 1 Scene 5, lines 134 to 141.

61 **if … dislike**: if you don't like either of them

	Unto the white-upturnèd wondering eyes	
	Of mortals that fall back to gaze on him	30
	When he bestrides the lazy-pacing clouds,	
	And sails upon the bosom of the air.	

JULIET   O Romeo, Romeo! Wherefore art thou Romeo?
Deny thy father and refuse thy name –
Or if thou wilt not, be but sworn my love   35
And I'll no longer be a Capulet.

ROMEO   (*Aside*) Shall I hear more, or shall I speak at this?

JULIET   'Tis but thy name that is my enemy.
Thou art thyself, though not a Montague.
What's 'Montague'? It is nor hand, nor foot,   40
Nor arm, nor face, nor any other part
Belonging to a man. O, be some other name!
What's in a name? That which we call a rose
By any other word would smell as sweet.
So Romeo would, were he not Romeo called,   45
Retain that dear perfection which he owes
Without that title. Romeo, doff thy name –
And for that name, which is no part of thee,
Take all myself.

ROMEO   I take thee at thy word.
Call me but love, and I'll be new-baptized.   50
Henceforth, I never will be Romeo.

JULIET   What man art thou, that thus bescreened in night
So stumblest on my counsel?

ROMEO   By a name
I know not how to tell thee who I am.
My name, dear saint, is hateful to myself   55
Because it is an enemy to thee.
Had I it written, I would tear the word.

JULIET   My ears have yet not drunk a hundred words
Of thy tongue's uttering, yet I know the sound.
Art thou not Romeo, and a Montague?   60

ROMEO   Neither, fair maid, if either thee dislike.

Juliet fears for Romeo's safety if he is caught in the garden. She says that she is uneasy because she has let him know that she loves him, but she is anxious to know whether he loves her in return.

66 **o'erperch**: fly over
67 **limits**: barriers

73 **proof ... enmity**: armoured against their hatred

76 **but**: unless

78 **proroguèd**: postponed / put off
    wanting of: lacking

81 **lent me counsel**: gave me advice
82 **pilot**: sailor / navigator
    wert thou: even if you were
83 **vast**: deserted
84 **adventure ... merchandise**: run the risk to gain goods like that
86 **Else**: otherwise

88 **Fain ... form**: I would gladly follow the traditional rules of courtship
89 **compliment**: polite social conventions

92 **perjuries**: lies / breaking of oaths
93 **Jove**: Jupiter, King of the gods

96 **say thee nay**: contradict you
97 **So ... woo**: so you have to go on courting me

Think about

• Juliet is worried that Romeo has heard her say that she loves him (lines 85 to 89). Why might it have been unwise for a girl in her situation to let a man know that she loved him?

• What does Juliet's speech (lines 85 to 106) reveal about her character, background and upbringing?

JULIET	How cam'st thou hither, tell me, and wherefore?
	The orchard walls are high and hard to climb –
	And the place death, considering who thou art,
	If any of my kinsmen find thee here.	**65**

ROMEO	With love's light wings did I o'erperch these walls,
	For stony limits cannot hold love out –
	And what love can do, that dares love attempt.
	Therefore thy kinsmen are no stop to me.

| JULIET | If they do see thee, they will murder thee. | **70** |

ROMEO	Alack, there lies more peril in thine eye
	Than twenty of their swords. Look thou but sweet
	And I am proof against their enmity.

| JULIET | I would not for the world they saw thee here. |

ROMEO	I have night's cloak to hide me from their eyes.	**75**
	And but thou love me, *let* them find me here.
	My life were better ended by their hate
	Than death proroguèd, wanting of thy love.

| JULIET | By whose direction found'st thou out this place? |

ROMEO	By love, that first did prompt me to inquire.	**80**
	He lent me counsel, and I lent him eyes.
	I am no pilot, yet wert thou as far
	As that vast shore washed with the farthest sea,
	I should adventure for such merchandise.

JULIET	Thou knowest the mask of night is on my face,	**85**
	Else would a maiden blush bepaint my cheek
	For that which thou hast heard me speak tonight.
	Fain would I dwell on form – fain, fain deny
	What I have spoke. – But farewell compliment!
	Dost thou love me? I know thou wilt say 'Ay' –	**90**
	And I will take thy word. Yet if thou swear'st
	Thou mayst prove false. At lovers' perjuries
	They say Jove laughs. O gentle Romeo,
	If thou dost love, pronounce it faithfully.
	Or if thou think I am too quickly won,	**95**
	I'll frown, and be perverse, and say thee nay,
	So thou wilt woo – but else, not for the world.

Romeo tries to declare his love for Juliet, but she is uneasy about the suddenness of their love.

Think about

- In this play, many different views of love are expressed, often through imagery. What do the images in the following lines suggest that love is: lines 109 to 111, 118 to 120, 121 to 122, and 133 to 134?

- How accurately does each of these images represent (a) Romeo's love for Juliet; and (b) her love for him?

98   **fond**: foolish
99   **'haviour light**: behaviour too forward

101   **cunning … strange**: cleverness in playing hard-to-get
103   **ere … ware**: before I realised

105   **not … love**: do not judge my surrender to be a sign of immodest love
106   **discoverèd**: revealed

109   **inconstant**: changeable
110   **circled orb**: the imagined sphere in which the moon moves

114   **idolatry**: idol-worship

117   **contract**: i.e. their exchange of lovers' promises
118   **rash**: hasty
       unadvised: ill-considered

129   **would it were**: wish I still had it
130   **Would'st … it**: Do you want to take it back

	In truth, fair Montague, I am too fond,	

In truth, fair Montague, I am too fond,
And therefore thou mayst think my 'haviour light.
But trust me, gentleman, I'll prove more true   100
Than those that have more cunning to be strange.
I should have been more strange, I must confess,
But that thou overheard'st, ere I was ware,
My true-love passion. Therefore pardon me,
And not impute this yielding to light love,   105
Which the dark night hath so discoverèd.

ROMEO Lady, by yonder blessèd moon I vow,
That tips with silver all these fruit-tree tops –

JULIET O swear not by the moon, th' inconstant moon,
That monthly changes in her circled orb,   110
Lest that thy love prove likewise variable.

ROMEO What shall I swear by?

JULIET   Do not swear at all. –
Or if thou wilt, swear by thy gracious self,
Which is the god of my idolatry,
And I'll believe thee.

ROMEO   If my heart's dear love –   115

JULIET Well, do not swear. Although I joy in thee,
I have no joy of this contract tonight.
It is too rash, too unadvised, too sudden –
Too like the lightning, which doth cease to be
Ere one can say 'It lightens'. Sweet, good night.   120
This bud of love, by summer's ripening breath,
May prove a beauteous flower when next we meet.
Good night, good night! As sweet repose and rest
Come to thy heart as that within my breast.

ROMEO O wilt thou leave me so unsatisfied?   125

JULIET What satisfaction canst thou have tonight?

ROMEO Th' exchange of thy love's faithful vow for mine.

JULIET I gave thee mine before thou didst request it –
And yet I would it were to give again.

ROMEO Would'st thou withdraw it? For what purpose, love?   130

Juliet hears the Nurse calling her. Before she goes, she asks Romeo to send her a message the following day telling her when and where they can be married.

Think about

- When Juliet returns to the window, she immediately talks of marriage (lines 142 to 148). Why might Juliet feel that she should marry Romeo as quickly as possible?

- What does Romeo mean by his statement about love and lovers (lines 156 to 157)? How effective is his comparison?

131 **frank**: generous

133 **bounty**: generosity and what I want to give you

137 **Anon**: I'm coming

141 **flattering-sweet**: delightful
substantial: real

143 **bent**: intention

145 **procure**: arrange
146 **rite**: marriage ceremony

151 **beseech**: beg
By and by: Straight away

152 **cease thy suit**: give up your courtship of me

155 **want**: lack

JULIET	But to be frank and give it thee again:
	And yet I wish but for the thing I have.
	My bounty is as boundless as the sea,
	My love as deep. The more I give to thee,
	The more I have, for both are infinite.	135

The NURSE *is heard calling from inside the house.*

	I hear some noise within. Dear love, adieu!
	– Anon, good Nurse! – Sweet Montague, be true.
	Stay but a little: I will come again.

She goes from the window.

ROMEO	O blessèd, blessèd night! I am afeard,
	Being in night, all this is but a dream,	140
	Too flattering-sweet to be substantial.

JULIET *returns above.*

JULIET	Three words, dear Romeo, and good night indeed.
	If that thy bent of love be honourable,
	Thy purpose marriage, send me word tomorrow
	By one that I'll procure to come to thee,	145
	Where and what time thou wilt perform the rite –
	And all my fortunes at thy foot I'll lay,
	And follow thee, my lord, throughout the world.

| NURSE | (*From inside the house*) Madam! |

| JULIET | I come! Anon! – But if thou mean'st not well, | 150 |
| | I do beseech thee – |

| NURSE | (*Calling again*) Madam! |

JULIET	By and by! I come!
	– To cease thy suit, and leave me to my grief.
	Tomorrow will I send.

| ROMEO | So thrive my soul, – |

| JULIET | A thousand times good night! |

She goes again.

ROMEO	A thousand times the worse, to want thy light!	155
	Love goes toward love as schoolboys from their books,
	But love from love, toward school with heavy looks.

Juliet returns and says she will send someone by nine in the morning for Romeo's message. The lovers are reluctant to part.

158 **Hist**: the sound a falconer makes to call a hawk

159 **tassel-gentle**: male falcon

160 **Bondage is hoarse**: i.e. being 'imprisoned' in the house, she has to whisper

161 **Echo**: a nymph in classical myth who pined away for love

166 **attending**: listening

166 **nyas**: a young hawk taken from its nest for training

172 **to**: in order to
still: always

Think about

• Look at the different set designs shown on pages 258 and 259. What does each one allow the actors to do? Which moments in this scene would be most effective (or hardest to achieve successfully) on each set?

• How does the language of falconry and bird-keeping help Romeo and Juliet to express their feelings here?

177 **wanton's bird**: spoilt child's pet bird

179 **gyves**: fetters / handcuffs

182 **would**: wish

He moves slowly away – as JULIET *returns once more to her window.*

JULIET	Hist, Romeo, hist! O for a falconer's voice,
	To lure this tassel-gentle back again.
	Bondage is hoarse, and may not speak aloud – **160**
	Else would I tear the cave where Echo lies,
	And make her airy tongue more hoarse than mine
	With repetition of my Romeo's name.

ROMEO   It is my soul that calls upon my name.
How silver-sweet sound lovers' tongues by night,   **165**
Like softest music to attending ears!

JULIET   Romeo!

ROMEO   My nyas?

JULIET   What o'clock tomorrow
Shall I send to thee?

ROMEO   By the hour of nine.

JULIET   I will not fail. 'Tis twenty years till then.
I have forgot why I did call thee back.   **170**

ROMEO   Let me stand here till thou remember it.

JULIET   I shall forget, to have thee still stand there,
Remembering how I love thy company.

ROMEO   And I'll still stay, to have thee still forget,
Forgetting any other home but this.   **175**

JULIET   'Tis almost morning. I would have thee gone –
And yet no farther than a wanton's bird,
Who lets it hop a little from her hand,
Like a poor prisoner in his twisted gyves,
And with a silk thread plucks it back again,   **180**
So loving-jealous of his liberty.

ROMEO   I would I were thy bird.

Juliet goes in and Romeo leaves, planning to seek advice and help from Friar Lawrence.

183 **much cherishing**: too much affection

188 **Hence will I**: I will go from here
ghostly ... cell: Friar Lawrence's hidden-away room
189 **crave**: ask for
hap: good fortune

Think about

- The phrase 'sweet sorrow' (line 184) is an oxymoron (an expression that seems to contradict itself while still making sense). In what ways does it represent Juliet's mixed feelings as she says goodbye? Look at lines 176 to 181, and 182 to 184, for example.

- In many productions Juliet seems much more practical than Romeo. What is there in this scene to support that interpretation?

JULIET
                                         Sweet, so would I –
Yet I should kill thee with much cherishing.
Good night, good night. Parting is such sweet sorrow,
That I shall say 'good night' till it be morrow.   **185**

                                                              She goes in.

ROMEO
Sleep dwell upon thine eyes, peace in thy breast.
Would I were sleep and peace, so sweet to rest!
Hence will I to my ghostly sire's close cell,
His help to crave, and my dear hap to tell.

                                                                      Exit.

RSC, 1995

National Theatre, 2000

Northern Broadsides, 1996

In this scene ...

- Romeo visits Friar Lawrence and tells him that he and Juliet have fallen in love.
- The Friar finally agrees to marry the couple, believing that their marriage will bring their two families together.

When Romeo arrives at Friar Lawrence's cell, the Friar is collecting plants and herbs which have medicinal properties.

3 **fleckled**: dappled with spots of light
4 **From ... wheels**: out of the way of the sun-god's chariot
5 **ere**: before
7 **osier cage**: willow basket
8 **baleful**: harmful
9–10 **that's ... womb**: is both the mother of all natural things and their grave
11 **divers kind**: various species
14 **None ... some**: there are no plants which do not have some good qualities
15 **mickle**: great
    powerful grace: i.e. healing power
17 **For ... vile**: For there is nothing, however lowly
19–20 **Nor aught ... abuse**: nor is there anything, however good, which will not turn away from its natural goodness if it is misused
22 **by action dignified**: can become good if it is used in the right way
23 **infant rind**: tender young skin
25 **that part**: the scent
    each part: each part of the body
26 **stays ... heart**: stops the heart and the senses too
27 **still**: always
28 **grace**: the ability to receive God's goodness
    rude will: giving in to physical desires
30 **canker**: caterpillar

---**Think about**---

- The Friar's speech (lines 1 to 30) contains many antitheses (opposites). What subjects do these relate to?

- Why do you think the language of this play is so full of opposites and contradictions?

Near Friar Lawrence's cell.

Enter FRIAR LAWRENCE, *alone, with a basket.*

FR. LAWRENCE	The grey-eyed morn smiles on the frowning night,
	Check'ring the eastern clouds with streaks of light;
	And fleckled darkness like a drunkard reels
	From forth day's path and Titan's fiery wheels.
	Now, ere the sun advance his burning eye 5
	The day to cheer and night's dank dew to dry,
	I must upfill this osier cage of ours
	With baleful weeds and precious-juicèd flowers.
	The earth that's nature's mother is her tomb:
	What is her burying grave, that is her womb. 10
	And from her womb children of divers kind
	We sucking on her natural bosom find:
	Many for many virtues excellent,
	None but for some, and yet all different.
	O, mickle is the powerful grace that lies 15
	In plants, herbs, stones, and their true qualities.
	For nought so vile that on the earth doth live
	But to the earth some special good doth give –
	Nor aught so good but, strained from that fair use,
	Revolts from true birth, stumbling on abuse. 20
	Virtue itself turns vice, being misapplied,
	And vice sometime by action dignified.

Enter ROMEO *behind (unseen by the* FRIAR).

	Within the infant rind of this weak flower
	Poison hath residence *and* medicine power.
	For this, being smelt, with that part cheers each part; 25
	Being tasted, stays all senses with the heart.
	Two such opposèd kings encamp them still
	In man as well as herbs – grace and rude will.
	And where the worser is predominant,
	Full soon the canker death eats up that plant. 30
ROMEO	Good morrow, father.

The Friar assumes that, because Romeo is up so early, he must have been with Rosaline. Romeo tells the Friar that he has fallen in love with Juliet, and asks the Friar to marry them.

31 **Benedicite**: God bless you

33 **argues ... head**: suggests that your mind is troubled

35 **Care ... eye**: Old men are kept awake by worries

37 **unbruisèd**: not yet injured by life
unstuffed: carefree

40 **uproused ... distemp'rature**: forced to get up early because you are troubled

46 **that name's woe**: the unhappiness that name caused me

Think about

• Look at Romeo's explanation about what has happened (lines 49 to 54). Why does Romeo use language about enemies and wounds to describe what he has been doing? What does he know about the character and interests of the person he is talking to?

• What does the Friar's reaction to Romeo's language (lines 55 to 56) suggest about him and his relationship with Romeo?

51–2 **Both ... lies**: Your help and holy medicine can be the remedy for both of us

54 **intercession ... foe**: request for help will benefit my enemy too

55 **homely in thy drift**: straightforward in the way you explain it

56 **Riddling ... shrift**: i.e. If you don't explain clearly, you won't receive proper forgiveness for your sins

63 **pass**: walk along together

67 **forsaken**: given up

FR. LAWRENCE	Benedicite!
	What early tongue so sweet saluteth me?
	Young son, it argues a distempered head
	So soon to bid good morrow to thy bed.
	Care keeps his watch in every old man's eye,
	And where care lodges, sleep will never lie –
	But where unbruisèd youth with unstuffed brain
	Doth couch his limbs, there golden sleep doth reign.
	Therefore thy earliness doth me assure
	Thou art uproused with some distemp'rature.
	Or if not so, then here I hit it right –
	Our Romeo hath not been in bed tonight.

FR. LAWRENCE   Benedicite!
What early tongue so sweet saluteth me?
Young son, it argues a distempered head
So soon to bid good morrow to thy bed.
Care keeps his watch in every old man's eye,   35
And where care lodges, sleep will never lie –
But where unbruisèd youth with unstuffed brain
Doth couch his limbs, there golden sleep doth reign.
Therefore thy earliness doth me assure
Thou art uproused with some distemp'rature.   40
Or if not so, then here I hit it right –
Our Romeo hath not been in bed tonight.

ROMEO   That last is true: the sweeter rest was mine.

FR. LAWRENCE God pardon sin! Wast thou with Rosaline?

ROMEO   With Rosaline, my ghostly father? No.   45
I have forgot that name, and that name's woe.

FR. LAWRENCE That's my good son. But where hast thou been then?

ROMEO   I'll tell thee ere thou ask it me again.
I have been feasting with mine enemy,
Where on a sudden one hath wounded me   50
That's by me wounded. Both our remedies
Within thy help and holy physic lies.
I bear no hatred, blessèd man; for lo,
My intercession likewise steads my foe.

FR. LAWRENCE Be plain, good son, and homely in thy drift;   55
Riddling confession finds but riddling shrift.

ROMEO   Then plainly know, my heart's dear love is set
On the fair daughter of rich Capulet.
As mine on hers, so hers is set on mine,
And all combined – save what thou must combine   60
By holy marriage. When and where and how
We met, we wooed, and made exchange of vow,
I'll tell thee as we pass. But this I pray,
That thou consent to marry us today.

FR. LAWRENCE Holy Saint Francis, what a change is here!   65
Is Rosaline that thou didst love so dear
So soon forsaken? Young men's love then lies

The Friar complains that Romeo is changeable in love, but agrees to help him.

69 **brine**: tears
70 **sallow**: pale

72 **season**: 1 give a flavour to; 2 preserve

79 **Pronounce this sentence**: Repeat this moral saying
80 **fall**: be excused for committing sins
81 **chid'st**: told me off
82 **doting**: being infatuated

86 **Doth ... allow**: i.e. Juliet returns Romeo's favour and love

88 **read by rote**: recited what it had learned by heart, i.e. Romeo had only imitated true love
90 **In one respect**: For one reason
92 **rancour**: bitter hatred

93 **stand**: insist

Think about

• Friar Lawrence says that he has told Romeo off 'for doting, not for loving' (line 82). What is the difference, and why is it important here?

• Why do you think the Friar agrees so readily to help Romeo? Look at lines 89 to 92. Do you think he is making the right decision?

Not truly in their hearts, but in their eyes.
Jesu Maria, what a deal of brine
Hath washed thy sallow cheeks for Rosaline!   70
How much salt water thrown away in waste
To season love, that of it doth not taste!
The sun not yet thy sighs from heaven clears,
Thy old groans ring yet in mine ancient ears –
Lo, here upon thy cheek the stain doth sit   75
Of an old tear that is not washed off yet.
If e'er thou wast thyself, and these woes thine,
Thou and these woes were all for Rosaline.
And art thou changed? Pronounce this sentence then:
Women may fall, when there's no strength in men.   80

ROMEO   Thou chid'st me oft for loving Rosaline.

FR. LAWRENCE   For doting, not for loving, pupil mine.

ROMEO   And bad'st me bury love.

FR. LAWRENCE   Not in a grave
To lay one in, another out to have.

ROMEO   I pray thee chide me not. Her I love now   85
Doth grace for grace and love for love allow.
The other did not so.

FR. LAWRENCE   O, she knew well
Thy love did read by rote that could not spell.
But come, young waverer, come go with me.
In one respect I'll thy assistant be –   90
For this alliance may so happy prove
To turn your households' rancour to pure love.

ROMEO   O let us hence. I stand on sudden haste!

FR. LAWRENCE   Wisely and slow. They stumble that run fast.

Exeunt.

RSC, 1984

Romeo and Juliet, 1996 (directed by B. Luhrmann)

RSC, 1995

RSC, 2000

In this scene ...

- Mercutio and Benvolio discuss Tybalt, who has sent Romeo a challenge to a duel.
- Romeo appears and enjoys some witty wordplay with Mercutio.
- The Nurse arrives, looking for Romeo. He gives her instructions about when and where Juliet is to meet him so that they can be married.

Mercutio and Benvolio wonder what has happened to Romeo. Benvolio says that Romeo has been sent a challenge by Tybalt, a skilled and deadly sword-fighter.

Think about

- In a performance, this exchange can be played as Mercutio either admiring or mocking Tybalt's skill as a fencer. If you were the director, which interpretation would you choose?

- What 'cause' (line 25) could Tybalt claim to justify challenging Romeo to a duel?

1   **should**: can
2   **tonight**: last night

9   **answer it**: accept the challenge
11–12 **how ... dared**: that, having been challenged, he is willing to fight
14   **white ... eye**: i.e. Rosaline has fair skin and dark eyes
15   **pin ... cleft**: i.e. centre of his heart, pierced
15–16 **blind bow-boy**: Cupid
16   **butt-shaft**: blunt practice arrow
18   **Why ... Tybalt**: What's so special about Tybalt
19   **Prince of Cats**: Tybalt was the cat's name in many old stories.
20   **captain of compliments**: master of polite ceremony
     pricksong: from sheet music, strictly following the notes
21   **proportion**: rhythm
22   **minim rests**: briefest pauses
23   **butcher ... button**: he is so accurate, he can slice an opponent's silk button
24   **of ... house**: from the finest school
25   **cause**: a reason for fighting, such as an insult to a man's honour
25–6 **passado ... hai**: fashionable terms for particular thrusts in fencing

A street in Verona.

Enter MERCUTIO *and* BENVOLIO.

MERCUTIO	Where the devil should this Romeo be? Came he not home tonight?
BENVOLIO	Not to his father's. I spoke with his man.
MERCUTIO	Why, that same pale hard-hearted wench, that Rosaline, torments him so, that he will sure run mad.
BENVOLIO	Tybalt, the kinsman to old Capulet, hath sent a letter to his father's house.
MERCUTIO	A challenge, on my life.
BENVOLIO	Romeo will answer it.
MERCUTIO	Any man that can write may answer a letter.
BENVOLIO	Nay, he will answer the letter's master, how he dares, being dared.
MERCUTIO	Alas, poor Romeo, he is already dead – stabbed with a white wench's black eye, run through the ear with a love song, the very pin of his heart cleft with the blind bow-boy's butt-shaft. And is he a man to encounter Tybalt?
BENVOLIO	Why, what is Tybalt?
MERCUTIO	More than Prince of Cats. O, he's the courageous captain of compliments! He fights as you sing pricksong – keeps time, distance, and proportion. He rests me his minim rests – one, two, and the third in your bosom. The very butcher of a silk button – a duellist, a duellist! – a gentleman of the very first house of the first and second cause. Ah, the immortal passado! – the punto reverso! – the 'hai'!
BENVOLIO	The what?

5

10

15

20

25

When Romeo arrives, Mercutio teases him, believing that he still longs for Rosaline. He complains that Romeo disappeared after the Capulet feast.

28 **The pox of**: A curse on
antic … fantasticoes: weird posers
29 **new tuners of accent**: trendy speakers
30 **tall**: brave
31 **grandsire**: grandfather
32 **strange flies**: foreign parasites
32–3 **fashion-mongers**: followers of fashion
33 **pardon-me's**: people with affected manners
33 **stand**: 1 insist on; 2 stand up
34 **form**: 1 way of doing something; 2 seat
34–5 **old bench**: i.e. old ways
37 **roe**: 1 deer (i.e. his girlfriend); 2 fish eggs (i.e. he looks thin)
38 **numbers**: poetry
39 **Petrarch**: a poet who wrote love sonnets to Laura
to his lady: compared to Rosaline
41–2 **Dido … Thisbe**: all heroines from famous love stories
41 **dowdy**: plain-looking woman
42 **hildings … harlots**: sluts … prostitutes
42–3 **a grey … purpose**: quite attractive, but hardly worth mentioning
44 **French slop**: style of baggy trousers
44–5 **gave … counterfeit**: deceived us
48 **slip**: counterfeit coins were called 'slips'
conceive: work it out
50 **strain courtesy**: forget good manners
51 **constrains**: forces
52 **bow … hams**: 1 bow; 2 have sex; 3 have a sexually transmitted disease
54 **most … it**: got the true meaning
56 **pink**: 1 perfection; 2 a small flower; 3 the hole-pattern in material
59 **pump well-flowered**: shoe well-decorated

Think about

• Nearly all Mercutio's examples of lovers (lines 41 to 43) came to tragic ends or caused tragedy. Why does he select them, rather than others, do you think? What does it suggest about him and his attitude to love?

| MERCUTIO | The pox of such antic, lisping, affecting fantasticoes! These new tuners of accent! – 'By Jesu, a very good blade!' 'A very tall man!' 'A very good whore!' – Why, is not this a lamentable thing, grandsire, that we should be thus afflicted with these strange flies, these fashion-mongers, these 'pardon-me's'! – who stand so much on the new form that they cannot sit at ease on the old bench? O, their bones, their bones! | 30 |
| | | 35 |

Enter ROMEO.

BENVOLIO	Here comes Romeo, here comes Romeo!	
MERCUTIO	Without his roe, like a dried herring. O flesh, flesh, how art thou fishified! Now is he for the numbers that Petrarch flowed in! Laura to his lady was a kitchen wench – marry, she had a better love to be-rhyme her – Dido a dowdy, Cleopatra a gipsy, Helen and Hero hildings and harlots, Thisbe a grey eye or so, but not to the purpose. Signior Romeo, bonjour! There's a French salutation to your French slop. You gave us the counterfeit fairly last night.	40
		45
ROMEO	Good morrow to you both. What counterfeit did I give you?	
MERCUTIO	The slip, sir, the slip! Can you not conceive?	
ROMEO	Pardon, good Mercutio. My business was great, and in such a case as mine a man may strain courtesy.	50
MERCUTIO	That's as much as to say, such a case as yours constrains a man to bow in the hams.	
ROMEO	Meaning to curtsy?	
MERCUTIO	Thou hast most kindly hit it.	
ROMEO	A most courteous exposition.	55
MERCUTIO	Nay, I am the very pink of courtesy.	
ROMEO	Pink for flower?	
MERCUTIO	Right.	
ROMEO	Why, then is my pump well-flowered.	

In a light-hearted mood Romeo and Mercutio enjoy some clever wordplay, each one trying to outdo the other.

Think about

- Lines 36 to 91 are full of wordplay that modern audiences are not likely to understand and productions often cut this section. What do you think is gained if it is cut, and what would be lost?

- What does this dialogue suggest about the relationship between the three men?

61 **single sole**: 1 thin sole of a shoe; 2 alone or single; 3 immortal soul

62–3 **solely singular**: 1 unique; 2 quite alone (and worn out)

66 **Switch ... match**: Make your horse go faster with whip and spurs, or I'll declare myself the winner

68 **wild-goose**: foolish and futile

69 **Was ... you**: Did I get even with you

72 **there ... goose**: 1 playing the fool; 2 looking for a prostitute

73 **bite ... ear**: a sign of affection (possibly ironic)

75 **sweeting ... sauce**: apple sauce (eaten with goose)

77–8 **here's ... broad**: i.e. you can make your tiny wit go a long way

80 **goose**: obvious fool

83 **by art**: i.e. by using your skill (with words)

84 **natural**: born idiot

85 **bauble**: 1 jester's stick; 2 penis

87 **tale**: 'tail' means penis (wordplay) **against the hair**: 1 against my wish; 2 pubic hair; 3 'hare' was a slang term for prostitute

88 **large**: 1 crude; 2 erect

90 **come**: to have an orgasm

91 **occupy**: i.e. have sex

MERCUTIO	Sure wit! Follow me this jest now till thou hast worn out thy pump – that when the single sole of it is worn, the jest may remain, after the wearing, solely singular.	60
ROMEO	O single-soled jest, solely singular for the singleness!	
MERCUTIO	Come between us, good Benvolio! My wit faints.	65
ROMEO	Switch and spurs, switch and spurs! – or I'll cry a match!	
MERCUTIO	Nay, if our wits run the wild-goose chase, I am done – for thou hast more of the wild-goose in one of thy wits than, I am sure, I have in my whole five. Was I with you there for the goose?	70
ROMEO	Thou wast never with me for anything when thou wast not there for the goose.	
MERCUTIO	I will bite thee by the ear for that jest.	
ROMEO	Nay, good goose, bite not.	
MERCUTIO	Thy wit is a very bitter sweeting. It is a most sharp sauce.	75
ROMEO	And is it not well served in to a sweet goose?	
MERCUTIO	O! – here's a wit of cheveril, that stretches from an inch narrow to an ell broad!	
ROMEO	I stretch it out for that word 'broad' – which, added to the 'goose', proves thee far and wide a broad goose.	80
MERCUTIO	Why, is not this better now than groaning for love? Now art thou sociable; now art thou Romeo! Now art thou what thou art, by art as well as by nature. For this drivelling love is like a great natural that runs lolling up and down to hide his bauble in a hole.	85
BENVOLIO	Stop there, stop there.	
MERCUTIO	Thou desirest me to stop in my tale against the hair.	
BENVOLIO	Thou wouldst else have made thy tale large.	
MERCUTIO	O, thou art deceived! I would have made it short, for I was come to the whole depth of my tale, and meant indeed to occupy the argument no longer.	90

The Nurse arrives with her servant, Peter, wanting to speak to Romeo.

92 **goodly gear**: i.e. a sight for sore eyes
A sail: the cry of sailors when a ship was sighted

93 **shirt … smock**: man and a woman

99 **God … e'en**: Good afternoon

100 **good e'en**: already past noon

101 **bawdy**: sexually vulgar
dial: clock

102 **prick**: 1 mark on a clock; 2 penis

103 **Out upon you**: Get away with you

105 **mar**: ruin

106–7 **quoth 'a**: did he say / indeed

111 **for fault of**: in the absence of

113 **Very well took**: well understood

115 **confidence**: private discussion; or perhaps she means 'conference' (talk)

116 **endite**: mockingly imitating the Nurse's mistake (line 115) he deliberately uses 'endite' for 'invite'

117 **bawd**: someone who arranges customers for prostitutes
So ho: a hunter's cry

118 **found**: got the scent of

119 **hare**: a slang term for prostitute
lenten pie: pie served without meat (in Lent)

120 **hoar**: 1 stale; 2 pronounced the same as 'whore'
spent: eaten up

Think about

• What does Romeo's cry of 'A sail' (line 92) suggest about the Nurse's costume and movement?

• Look at the photographs of the Nurse from different productions (pages 126 and 127). What would she look like if you were directing the play? Think about how old she would be and how she would be dressed, for example.

Enter the NURSE, *with* PETER, *a servant.*

ROMEO	Here's goodly gear! A sail, a sail!
MERCUTIO	Two, two! A shirt and a smock.
NURSE	Peter!
PETER	Anon.
NURSE	My fan, Peter.
MERCUTIO	Good Peter, to hide her face – for her fan's the fairer face.
NURSE	God ye good morrow, gentlemen.
MERCUTIO	God ye good e'en, fair gentlewoman.
NURSE	Is it good e'en?
MERCUTIO	'Tis no less, I tell ye. For the bawdy hand of the dial is now upon the prick of noon.
NURSE	Out upon you! What a man are you?
ROMEO	One, gentlewoman, that God hath made – for himself to mar.
NURSE	By my troth, it is well said. 'For himself to mar', quoth 'a! Gentlemen, can any of you tell me where I may find the young Romeo?
ROMEO	I can tell you, but young Romeo will be older when you have found him than he was when you sought him. I am the youngest of that name, for fault of a worse.
NURSE	You say well.
MERCUTIO	Yea, is the worst well? Very well took, i' faith: wisely, wisely.
NURSE	If you be he, sir, I desire some confidence with you.
BENVOLIO	She will endite him to some supper.
MERCUTIO	A bawd, a bawd, a bawd! So ho!
ROMEO	What hast thou found?
MERCUTIO	No hare, sir – unless a hare, sir, in a lenten pie, that is something stale and hoar ere it be spent.

95

100

105

110

115

120

Mercutio mocks the Nurse with sexual jokes before leaving with Benvolio. The Nurse complains to Romeo about Mercutio's treatment of her.

123 **meat**: slang for 'prostitute'

125 **too … score**: not worth paying for

126 **hoars**: 1 gets stale; 2 spends time with whores
spent: finished up

131 **saucy merchant**: rude / insolent character

132 **ropery**: vulgar jokes

134 **stand to**: 1 live up to; 2 be sexually aroused

136 **take him down**: humiliate him (but with an unintended sexual meaning)

137 **an … lustier**: even if he were livelier
Jacks: rogues

138 **Scurvy**: Rotten

139 **flirt-gills**: immoral women
skains-mates: brawling friends

140 **suffer**: permit

141 **use … pleasure**: 1 make rude fun of me; 2 have casual sex with me

143 **weapon**: 1 sword; 2 penis

146 **vexed**: irritated

150–1 **lead … paradise**: take advantage of her innocence

151 **gross**: bad / wicked

Think about

• Do you find Mercutio's language when talking to the Nurse (lines 117 to 130) funny, or offensively sexist and insulting to her age?

• What is your opinion of Romeo's treatment of the Nurse here?

He walks around the NURSE, *singing.*

> An old hare hoar,
> And an old hare hoar,
> Is very good meat in Lent:
> But a hare that is hoar
> Is too much for a score,   125
> When it hoars ere it be spent.

Romeo, will you come to your father's? We'll to dinner thither.

ROMEO   I will follow you.

MERCUTIO   Farewell, ancient lady. Farewell, lady – (*singing again*)
lady, lady.   130

> *Exit, with* BENVOLIO.

NURSE   I pray you, sir, what saucy merchant was this that was so full of his ropery?

ROMEO   A gentleman, Nurse, that loves to hear himself talk, and will speak more in a minute than he will stand to in a month.   135

NURSE   And 'a stand to anything against me, I'll take him down, an 'a were lustier than he is – and twenty such Jacks! And if I cannot, I'll find those that shall. Scurvy knave! I am none of his flirt-gills, I am none of his skains-mates! (*To* PETER) And thou must stand by, too, and suffer every 140 knave to use me at his pleasure!

PETER   I saw no man use you at his pleasure. If I had, my weapon should quickly have been out. I warrant you, I dare draw as soon as another man if I see occasion in a good quarrel, and the law on my side.   145

NURSE   Now, afore God, I am so vexed that every part about me quivers! – Scurvy knave! – (*To* ROMEO) Pray you, sir, a word. And, as I told you, my young lady bid me inquire you out. What she bid me say I will keep to myself. But first let me tell ye, if ye should lead her into a fool's 150 paradise, as they say, it were a very gross kind of behaviour, as they say. For the gentlewoman is young –

Romeo instructs the Nurse to tell Juliet to meet him at the Friar's cell that afternoon, where they will be married. Meanwhile his servant will supply a rope-ladder so that Romeo can climb up to Juliet's room that night.

153 **deal double with**: double-cross

155 **weak dealing**: mean behaviour

156 **commend**: remember
     protest: swear / declare (can mean 'declare my love')

160 **mark me**: take notice of what I say

164 **shrift**: confession

166 **shrived**: confessed
     thy pains: your trouble

170 **stay**: wait

172 **tackled stair**: rope-ladder
173 **high topgallant**: highest point on a ship
174 **convoy**: means of access
175 **quit thy pains**: reward you for your trouble

179 **secret**: trustworthy
180 **Two … away**: Two people – minus one – can keep a secret (i.e. keep it to yourself)
181 **warrant**: assure

---Think about

• The Nurse has come to bring a message from Juliet, but what comment does she add of her own (lines 147 to 155)? What point is she making to Romeo and why does she make it?

• What is your view of the fact that both the Friar and the Nurse are acting in ways that encourage Romeo and Juliet to behave hastily?

	and therefore, if you should deal double with her, truly it were an ill thing to be offered to any gentlewoman, and very weak dealing.	155
ROMEO	Nurse, commend me to thy lady and mistress. I protest unto thee –	
NURSE	Good heart! And i' faith I will tell her as much. Lord, Lord, she will be a joyful woman!	
ROMEO	What wilt thou tell her, Nurse? Thou dost not mark me.	160
NURSE	I will tell her, sir, that you do protest – which, as I take it, is a gentleman-like offer.	
ROMEO	Bid her devise Some means to come to shrift this afternoon. And there she shall, at Friar Lawrence's cell, Be shrived and married. (*Offering money*) Here is for thy pains.	165
NURSE	No, truly, sir: not a penny.	
ROMEO	Go to, I say you shall.	
NURSE	(*Taking the money*) This afternoon, sir? Well, she shall be there.	
ROMEO	And stay, good Nurse, behind the abbey wall. Within this hour my man shall be with thee, And bring thee cords made like a tackled stair, Which to the high topgallant of my joy Must be my convoy in the secret night. Farewell. Be trusty, and I'll quit thy pains. Farewell. Commend me to thy mistress.	170
		175
NURSE	Now God in heaven bless thee! Hark you, sir.	
ROMEO	What say'st thou, my dear Nurse?	
NURSE	Is your man secret? Did you ne'er hear say, 'Two may keep counsel, putting one away'?	180
ROMEO	I warrant thee, my man's as true as steel.	

Before leaving, the Nurse tells
Romeo that Count Paris wants to
marry Juliet.

183 **prating**: chattering

184–5 **would … aboard**: would very much
like to marry her

185 **as lief**: as soon

187 **properer**: more handsome

188 **clout**: sheet

189 **versal**: universal / entire
rosemary: the herb of remembrance
(used at Elizabethan weddings and
funerals)

192 **the dog's name**: 'R' was called the
dog's letter, possibly because it sounds
like a dog growling.

194 **sententious**: she probably means
'sentences' (moral sayings)

199 **Before**: Walk in front of me
apace: get a move on

Think about

• What has to happen
between this point (noon)
and midnight to further
Romeo and Juliet's
happiness? Think about the
roles of (a) the Friar; (b) the
Nurse; and (c) Romeo's
man.

• What is the effect when we
hear the Nurse mention
Paris here?

NURSE	Well, sir. My mistress is the sweetest lady. Lord, Lord! – when 'twas a little prating thing – O, there is a nobleman in town, one Paris, that would fain lay knife aboard – but she, good soul, had as lief see a toad, a **185** very toad, as see him. I anger her, sometimes, and tell her that Paris is the properer man – but I'll warrant you, when I say so, she looks as pale as any clout in the versal world. Doth not 'rosemary' and 'Romeo' begin with a letter? **190**
ROMEO	Ay, Nurse, what of that? Both with an R.
NURSE	Ah, mocker! That's the dog's name. R is for the – No, I know it begins with some other letter. And she hath the prettiest sententious of it, of you and rosemary, that it would do you good to hear it. **195**
ROMEO	Commend me to thy lady.
NURSE	Ay, a thousand times. Peter!
PETER	Anon.
NURSE	(*Handing him her fan*) Before, and apace.

Exeunt.

In this scene ...

- When the Nurse returns to Juliet, she keeps putting off giving Romeo's message, complaining of tiredness.
- She finally tells Juliet when and where she is to meet Romeo and be married.

Juliet waits at home, impatient for the return of the Nurse. She finally arrives, moaning about her exhausting errand.

3 **Perchance**: perhaps
4 **heralds**: messengers

6 **louring**: gloomy / threatening
7 **nimble-pinioned**: swift-winged
   draw Love: pull Venus's chariot

12 **affections**: feelings

14 **bandy**: strike (with a racket)

16 **feign ... were**: act as if they were
17 **Unwieldy**: clumsy

Think about

- Juliet's language reflects her mood. What words or phrases in lines 1 to 17 give an idea of movement? What do you notice about the length of line 15, for example? What does this speech reveal about her feelings?

- What picture do you form in your mind from Juliet's image in lines 12 to 15? In what ways does the image add to the contrast made throughout the play between youth and age?

25 **give me leave**: leave me alone
26 **What ... have I**: What a tiring journey I've had

The Capulet garden.

Enter JULIET.

JULIET   The clock struck nine when I did send the Nurse –
In half an hour she promised to return.
Perchance she cannot meet him – that's not so.
O, she is lame! Love's heralds should be thoughts,
Which ten times faster glides than the sun's beams   5
Driving back shadows over louring hills.
Therefore do nimble-pinioned doves draw Love,
And therefore hath the wind-swift Cupid wings.
Now is the sun upon the highmost hill
Of this day's journey, and from nine to twelve   10
Is three long hours – yet she is not come.
Had she affections and warm youthful blood,
She would be as swift in motion as a ball:
My words would bandy her to my sweet love,
And his to me.   15
But old folks – many feign as they were dead:
Unwieldy, slow, heavy, and pale as lead.

Enter PETER, *followed by the* NURSE.

     O God, she comes! – O honey Nurse, what news?
Hast thou met with him? Send thy man away.

NURSE   Peter, stay at the gate.   20

                                   Exit PETER.

JULIET   Now good sweet Nurse – O Lord, why look'st thou sad?
Though news be sad, yet tell them merrily.
If good, thou sham'st the music of sweet news
By playing it to me with so sour a face.

NURSE   I am aweary: give me leave a while.   25
Fie, how my bones ache! What a jaunce have I!

JULIET   I would thou hadst my bones, and I thy news.
Nay, come, I pray thee, speak: good, good Nurse, speak.

Juliet becomes increasingly impatient as the Nurse delays telling her what Romeo said.

Think about

- Look at the Nurse's comments on Romeo in lines 38 to 44. Why do you think she expresses her opinions on him in this roundabout way?

- If you were the director, how would you want Juliet to react and what would you want her to do while the Nurse gets around to giving her the news? Look at line 50, for example.

29   **stay**: wait

34   **excuse**: make excuses for not telling

36   **stay the circumstance**: wait for the details

38   **simple**: foolish

42   **be not ... on**: are not worth talking about

44   **Go thy ... God**: Off you go, girl: be good

50   **a' t'other**: on the other

51   **Beshrew**: Curse

52   **jauncing**: trudging

53   **I' faith**: I promise you

55   **honest**: honourable

58   **within**: indoors

62   **hot**: impatient (perhaps also 'eager for Romeo')
     Marry ... trow: i.e. What a way to behave

63   **poultice**: cure (dressing used to ease aches)

NURSE	Jesu, what haste! Can you not stay a while?
	Do you not see that I am out of breath?	30

NURSE   Jesu, what haste! Can you not stay a while?
Do you not see that I am out of breath?   30

JULIET   How art thou out of breath, when thou hast breath
To say to me that thou art out of breath?
The excuse that thou dost make in this delay
Is longer than the tale thou dost excuse.
Is thy news good or bad? Answer to that.   35
Say either, and I'll stay the circumstance.
Let me be satisfied: is't good or bad?

NURSE   Well, you have made a simple choice – you know not
how to choose a man. Romeo? No, not he. Though his
face be better than any man's, yet his leg excels all   40
men's – and for a hand and a foot and a body, though
they be not to be talked on, yet they are past compare.
He is not the flower of courtesy, but, I'll warrant him, as
gentle as a lamb. Go thy ways, wench: serve God.
What, have you dined at home?   45

JULIET   No, no! But all this did I know before!
What says he of our marriage? What of that?

NURSE   Lord, how my head aches! What a head have I!
It beats as it would fall in twenty pieces.
My back a' t'other side – ah, my back, my back!   50
Beshrew your heart for sending me about
To catch my death with jauncing up and down!

JULIET   I' faith, I am sorry that thou art not well.
Sweet, sweet, sweet Nurse, tell me – what says my love?

NURSE   Your love says, like an honest gentleman, and a   55
courteous, and a kind, and a handsome, and, I warrant,
a virtuous – Where is your mother?

JULIET   Where is my mother? Why, she is within.
Where should she be? How oddly thou repliest!
– 'Your love says, like an honest gentleman,   60
"Where is your mother?"'

NURSE   O God's lady dear!
Are you so hot? Marry, come up, I trow!
Is this the poultice for my aching bones?
Henceforth do your messages yourself.

The Nurse finally tells Juliet that she must meet Romeo at the Friar's cell and be married that afternoon. Meanwhile the Nurse will fetch the rope-ladder.

65   **coil**: fuss

66   **shrift**: confession

68   **hie you hence**: hurry off

70   **wanton**: playful / uncontrolled
71   **They'll ... straight**: your cheeks blush very readily

75   **drudge**: poor servant
      toil: labour / work hard
76   **bear the burden**: i.e. carry Romeo's weight

---Think about---

• In her final speech the Nurse restates her plan. How effective is this as an ending to the scene?

• From what you know so far, how would you describe (a) the Nurse's feelings for Juliet; (b) her attitude towards Juliet's mother; and (c) her role and position in the Capulet household?

| JULIET | Here's such a coil! Come, what says Romeo? | 65 |

| NURSE | Have you got leave to go to shrift today? | |

| JULIET | I have. | |

NURSE	Then hie you hence to Friar Lawrence' cell.	
	There stays a husband to make you a wife.	
	Now comes the wanton blood up in your cheeks:	70
	They'll be in scarlet straight at any news.	
	Hie you to church! I must another way,	
	To fetch a ladder – by the which your love	
	Must climb a bird's nest soon when it is dark.	
	I am the drudge, and toil in your delight,	75
	But you shall bear the burden soon at night.	
	Go! I'll to dinner. Hie you to the cell.	

| JULIET | Hie to high fortune! Honest Nurse, farewell. | |

Exeunt.

RSC, 1986

RSC, 1995

RSC, 1989

Northern Broadsides, 1996

In this scene ...

• The Friar advises Romeo about the nature of love.

• Juliet arrives and she and Romeo go off to be married.

The Friar warns Romeo about the short lifespan of sudden and violent love, and then Juliet arrives.

Think about

• Why are lines 1 to 2, and 7 to 8 examples of dramatic irony (a situation in which the audience knows something which the character does not)? Think about the Prologue to Act 1. How might these lines make the audience feel?

• What three images does the Friar use to persuade Romeo to 'love moderately' (lines 9 to 15)? How effective do you find them?

2 **That ... not**: so that the future does not punish us with unhappiness

3 **But come ... can**: I don't care what sorrow comes

4 **countervail**: equal

6 **Do ... close**: Simply join

8 **but**: simply / only

10 **powder**: gunpowder

12 **Is loathsome ... deliciousness**: can become sickly and disgusting

13 **confounds**: destroys

15 **Too swift ... slow**: i.e. more haste, less speed

16–17 **so light ... flint**: i.e. her feet are barely touching the ground

18 **bestride the gossamers**: ride on spiders' threads

19 **idles**: floats around
    wanton: playful

20 **vanity**: the delights of this world (compared with his religion)

21 **ghostly**: spiritual

23 **As ... him**: I must give him a kiss in return

24–5 **if the ... mine**: if you are feeling as much happiness as I am

25 **that**: if

26 **blazon**: richly describe

Friar Lawrence's cell.

Enter FRIAR LAWRENCE, *with* ROMEO.

FR. LAWRENCE	So smile the heavens upon this holy act
	That after-hours with sorrow chide us not!

ROMEO   Amen, amen! But come what sorrow can,
It cannot countervail the exchange of joy
That one short minute gives me in her sight.   5
Do thou but close our hands with holy words,
Then love-devouring death do what he dare.
It is enough I may but call her mine.

FR. LAWRENCE   These violent delights have violent ends,
And in their triumph die – like fire and powder,   10
Which, as they kiss, consume. The sweetest honey
Is loathsome in his own deliciousness,
And in the taste confounds the appetite.
Therefore, love moderately. Long love doth so:
Too swift arrives as tardy as too slow.   15

JULIET *enters, hurriedly, and embraces* ROMEO.

Here comes the lady. O, so light a foot
Will ne'er wear out the everlasting flint.
A lover may bestride the gossamers
That idles in the wanton summer air,
And yet not fall, so light is vanity.   20

JULIET   Good even to my ghostly confessor.

FR. LAWRENCE   Romeo shall thank thee, daughter, for us both.

ROMEO *kisses her.*

JULIET   As much to him – else is his thanks too much.

She returns his kiss.

ROMEO   Ah, Juliet, if the measure of thy joy
Be heaped like mine, and that thy skill be more   25
To blazon it, then sweeten with thy breath

Romeo and Juliet declare their love for one another and the Friar leads them off to be married.

28 **Unfold**: i.e. describe
29 **in either**: from the other person
   dear encounter: precious meeting
30 **Conceit**: Understanding
   matter: content
31 **substance**: true meaning
   ornament: flowery language
32 **They are ... worth**: If you can say how much money you've got, you're not really rich
34 **sum up sum**: calculate the total
36 **by your leaves**: with your permission

┌─ **Think about**
│ • How would you describe the language Juliet uses to describe her love in lines 30 to 34? What does it reveal about her?

This neighbour air – and let rich music's tongue
Unfold the imagined happiness that both
Receive in either, by this dear encounter.

JULIET   Conceit more rich in matter than in words   30
Brags of his substance, not of ornament.
They are but beggars that can count their worth –
But my true love is grown to such excess
I cannot sum up sum of half my wealth.

FR. LAWRENCE Come, come with me, and we will make short work –   35
For, by your leaves, you shall not stay alone
Till Holy Church incorporate two in one.

Exeunt.

In this scene ...

- Mercutio and Benvolio meet Tybalt, who is looking for Romeo.
- Tybalt insults Romeo. When he does not respond, Mercutio angrily challenges Tybalt himself.
- Mercutio and Tybalt fight. Mercutio is fatally wounded.
- Feeling ashamed that Mercutio has died on his behalf, Romeo fights with Tybalt and kills him.
- As punishment, the Prince exiles Romeo from Verona.

Benvolio is anxious about walking the streets when the Capulets are likely to be around. Mercutio teases Benvolio, accusing him of being a quarreller himself.

1 **retire**: get off the streets
2 **Capels are abroad**: Capulets are out and about
3 **scape**: avoid

6 **claps ... sword**: bangs his sword down

8 **operation ... cup**: time his second glass of wine has taken effect
8–9 **draws ... drawer**: draws his sword on the barman
11 **Jack**: fellow
12–13 **as soon ... moved**: as quickly moved to anger and as angry at being provoked

15 **two such**: two people like you

Think about

- How does Shakespeare create tension in the opening of this scene?

- Benvolio's name means something like 'well-wishing'. What does he say here which suggests that he is a peace-maker? Where else in the play has he shown that quality?

20 **hazel**: 1 a nut; 2 an eye colour

22 **meat**: food / nourishment
23 **addle**: rotten (as a bad egg)

27 **doublet**: jacket
before Easter: traditionally the time for bringing out new fashions
28 **riband**: laces
29 **tutor ... quarrelling**: teach *me* not to quarrel

A square in Verona.

Enter MERCUTIO *and* BENVOLIO, *with other Montague servants and Mercutio's page.*

BENVOLIO	I pray thee, good Mercutio, let's retire.
	The day is hot, the Capels are abroad,
	And if we meet we shall not scape a brawl –
	For now, these hot days, is the mad blood stirring.

MERCUTIO Thou art like one of these fellows that, when he enters   5
the confines of a tavern, claps me his sword upon the
table and says 'God send me no need of thee!' – and,
by the operation of the second cup draws him on the
drawer, when indeed there *is* no need.

BENVOLIO Am *I* like such a fellow?   10

MERCUTIO Come, come. Thou art as hot a Jack in thy mood as any
in Italy, and as soon moved to be moody – and as soon
moody to be moved.

BENVOLIO And what to?

MERCUTIO Nay, and there were two such, we should have none   15
shortly, for one would kill the other. Thou? Why, thou
wilt quarrel with a man that hath a hair more or a hair
less in his beard than thou hast! Thou wilt quarrel with
a man for cracking nuts, having no other reason but
because thou hast hazel eyes. What eye but such an eye   20
would spy out such a quarrel? Thy head is as full of
quarrels as an egg is full of meat, and yet thy head hath
been beaten as addle as an egg for quarrelling. Thou
hast quarrelled with a man for coughing in the street
because he hath wakened thy dog that hath lain asleep   25
in the sun! Didst thou not fall out with a tailor for
wearing his new doublet before Easter? With another for
tying his new shoes with old riband? And yet thou wilt
tutor *me* from quarrelling!

Tybalt appears with some other Capulets. Mercutio provokes Tybalt, but Tybalt is looking for Romeo. When Romeo arrives, Tybalt calls him a villain.

30 And: If
31 fee-simple: absolute ownership (his life would be cheap, because it would be very short)
32 simple: stupid

33 By my head: a common oath

34 By my heel: a scornful oath invented by Mercutio

39 apt enough to: ready for
    an: if
40 occasion: reason

42 consortest with: are often in the company of
43 Consort: group of musicians
    minstrels: paid musicians, i.e. no better than servants
45 fiddlestick: i.e. his sword
46 Zounds: By God's wounds (an oath)
47 haunt: place / thoroughfare
49 reason … grievances: discuss your differences calmly
50 depart: go your separate ways

Think about

• What different motivations do the three characters have here? Think about why Tybalt approaches Mercutio and what he wants, whether Mercutio is trying to provoke a fight and why he might want to, and what Benvolio is trying to do.

54 livery: servant's uniform (i.e. he isn't your servant)
55 go … field: walk in front of him to the duelling field
56 'man': i.e. a man of honour (willing to fight a duel)
58 thou … villain: a direct insult that would lead to a duel

BENVOLIO	And I were so apt to quarrel as thou art, any man should 30 buy the fee-simple of my life for an hour and a quarter.
MERCUTIO	The fee-simple? O, simple!

Enter TYBALT, *with other Capulets and servants.*

BENVOLIO	By my head, here come the Capulets!
MERCUTIO	By my heel, I care not.
TYBALT	(*To his men*) Follow me close, for I will speak to them. 35 (*To* MERCUTIO *and* BENVOLIO) Gentlemen, good e'en: a word with one of you.
MERCUTIO	And but one word with one of us? Couple it with something. Make it a word and a blow.
TYBALT	You shall find me apt enough to that, sir, an you will give me occasion. 40
MERCUTIO	Could you not take some occasion without giving?
TYBALT	Mercutio, thou consortest with Romeo –
MERCUTIO	Consort? What, dost thou make us minstrels? And thou make minstrels of us, look to hear nothing but discords. Here's *my* fiddlestick! (*Moving his hand to his sword*) – 45 Here's that shall make you dance. Zounds, consort!
BENVOLIO	We talk here in the public haunt of men! Either withdraw unto some private place, Or reason coldly of your grievances, Or else depart. Here, all eyes gaze on us. 50
MERCUTIO	Men's eyes were made to look, and let them gaze. I will not budge for no man's pleasure, I.

Enter ROMEO.

TYBALT	Well, peace be with you, sir. Here comes my man.
MERCUTIO	But I'll be hanged, sir, if he wear your livery. Marry, go before to field, he'll be your follower – 55 Your worship in that sense may call him 'man'.
TYBALT	Romeo, the love I bear thee can afford No better term than this: thou art a villain.

Romeo responds calmly to Tybalt's insults and tries to make peace with him. Mercutio disapproves of Romeo's attitude and challenges Tybalt. They fight and Mercutio is wounded.

Think about

- There are different ways in which Tybalt could try to provoke Romeo. In the Luhrmann film, for example, Tybalt kicks him to the ground and injures him. What would you have Tybalt do if you were the director?

- How would you describe the tone of Romeo's replies to Tybalt? What does Mercutio think of Romeo's response?

60–1 **Doth … greeting**: excuses me for not displaying the anger appropriate to your greeting

63 **Boy**: another serious insult

65 **protest**: promise / declare
66 **devise**: understand

68 **tender**: value

71 **Alla stoccata**: At the thrust (a fencing term)
carries it away: has won (i.e. is the right thing to say now)
72 **rat-catcher**: i.e. he is 'King of Cats'
will you walk: a challenge to a duel
74 **nine lives**: Cats are said to have nine lives.
75 **make bold withal**: do what I want with
75–6 **as you … eight**: depending how you behave to me afterwards, I'll thrash the other eight
77 **his pilcher**: its sheath (insulting)
by the ears: forcefully
78 **about your ears**: attacking you
80 **put … up**: put your sword away
81 **passado**: lunge
83 **forbear**: stop

85 **bandying**: exchanging blows

ROMEO	Tybalt, the reason that I have to love thee
	Doth much excuse the appertaining rage 60
	To such a greeting. Villain am I none.
	Therefore, farewell. I see thou know'st me not.
TYBALT	Boy, this shall not excuse the injuries
	That thou hast done me. Therefore turn, and draw!
ROMEO	I do protest I never injured thee, 65
	But love thee better than thou canst devise –
	Till thou shalt know the reason of my love.
	And so, good Capulet – which name I tender
	As dearly as mine own – be satisfied.
MERCUTIO	O calm, dishonourable, vile submission! 70
	'Alla stoccata' carries it away! (*Drawing his sword*)
	Tybalt, you rat-catcher, will you walk?
TYBALT	What wouldst thou have with me?
MERCUTIO	Good King of Cats, nothing but one of your nine lives
	that I mean to make bold withal – and, as you shall use 75
	me hereafter, dry-beat the rest of the eight. Will you
	pluck your sword out of his pilcher by the ears? Make
	haste, lest mine be about your ears ere it be out.
TYBALT	(*Drawing his sword*) I am for you!
ROMEO	Gentle Mercutio, put thy rapier up. 80
MERCUTIO	(*To* TYBALT) Come, sir, your passado!

MERCUTIO *and* TYBALT *fight.*

ROMEO	Draw, Benvolio! Beat down their weapons!
	Gentlemen, for shame, forbear this outrage!
	Tybalt! Mercutio! The Prince expressly hath
	Forbid this bandying in Verona streets. 85
	Hold, Tybalt! Good Mercutio!

ROMEO *comes between them, obstructing the fight.* TYBALT *makes a hidden thrust past* ROMEO's *body, and wounds* MERCUTIO.

Exit TYBALT, *running, with his followers.*

The dying Mercutio curses the families for their feud. Left alone, Romeo feels ashamed that he did not respond to Tybalt's insults himself. Benvolio returns to announce that Mercutio is dead.

87 **houses**: families
   sped: finished (i.e. fatally wounded)
88 **and hath nothing**: without being wounded in return
89 **a scratch**: i.e. it was inflicted by the 'King of Cats'

93 **'twill serve**: it'll do / it will be enough (i.e. to kill me)
94 **grave**: 1 serious (unusual for him); 2 buried in a grave
94–5 **peppered ... world**: finished as far as this world is concerned
96 **Zounds**: God's wounds
97 **braggart**: boaster
98 **book of arithmetic**: rule book
103 **worms' meat**: a corpse (only fit to be eaten by worms)
103–4 **I have ... too**: I am wounded, and fatally

105 **near ally**: close relative
106 **very**: true

108 **slander**: insulting words

110 **effeminate**: lacking manly virtues
111 **temper**: 1 character; 2 hardening of steel
   softened ... steel: weakened my courage
113 **aspired**: soared up to
114 **untimely**: early / prematurely

Think about

- In the Luhrmann film, Mercutio realises that he is seriously wounded after line 94, but in the 1983 RSC production it was not until line 98. Where do you think is the most effective point?

- Does Mercutio seem to blame Tybalt, Romeo, or the feud between the families the most for his death? Where do you think the blame lies?

- Many people in Shakespeare's time believed that a dying man's curse was certain to be fulfilled. Why is that superstition significant here?

MERCUTIO	I am hurt.
	A plague o' both your houses! I am sped.
	Is he gone, and hath nothing?

| BENVOLIO | What, art thou hurt? |

| MERCUTIO | Ay, ay, a scratch, a scratch. Marry, 'tis enough. |
| | Where is my page? Go, villain, fetch a surgeon.   90 |

Exit the page, running.

| ROMEO | Courage, man: the hurt cannot be much. |

MERCUTIO	No, 'tis not so deep as a well, nor so wide as a church
	door – but 'tis enough, 'twill serve. Ask for me tomorrow
	and you shall find me a grave man. I am peppered, I
	warrant, for this world. A plague, o' both your houses! 95
	Zounds! A dog, a rat, a mouse, a cat – to scratch a man
	to death! A braggart, a rogue, a villain that fights by the
	book of arithmetic! Why the devil came you between
	us? I was hurt under your arm.

| ROMEO | I thought all for the best.   100 |

MERCUTIO	Help me into some house, Benvolio,
	Or I shall faint. A plague o' both your houses!
	They have made worms' meat of me. I have it,
	And soundly too. – Your houses!

Exit, supported by BENVOLIO.

ROMEO	This gentleman, the Prince's near ally, 105
	My very friend, hath got this mortal hurt
	In *my* behalf: my reputation stained
	With Tybalt's slander. – Tybalt! – that an hour
	Hath been my cousin. O sweet Juliet –
	Thy beauty hath made me effeminate, 110
	And in my temper softened valour's steel!

Re-enter BENVOLIO.

BENVOLIO	O Romeo, Romeo! Brave Mercutio is dead!
	That gallant spirit hath aspired the clouds,
	Which too untimely here did scorn the earth.

When Tybalt returns, Romeo kills him. He flees before the Prince arrives with the Montagues and Capulets.

115 on more … depend: i.e. threatens the future with more unhappiness

119 respective lenity: gentleness which comes from respect (perhaps for the Prince's laws, or his new relationship with Tybalt)
120 be my conduct: guide my actions
124 Staying: waiting

126 consort: accompany

129 up: raised up and in arms
130 amazed: in a daze
doom thee death: sentence you to death
131 taken: arrested
132 fortune's fool: i.e. a plaything or helpless victim of the goddess Fortune

---
Think about

• In what ways should the fight between Romeo and Tybalt be different from the earlier one between Mercutio and Tybalt? Think about the differences between Romeo's and Mercutio's moods as they approach their fights, for example.

• What does Romeo mean by 'O, I am fortune's fool' (line 132)? What might he be thinking or feeling at this moment?

136 charge: order

ROMEO	This day's black fate on more days doth depend: 115
	This but begins the woe others must end.

Re-enter TYBALT.

BENVOLIO	Here comes the furious Tybalt back again.
ROMEO	Alive – in triumph! And Mercutio slain!
	Away to heaven, respective lenity,
	And fire-eyed fury be my conduct now! 120
	Now, Tybalt, take the 'villain' back again
	That late thou gavest me – for Mercutio's soul
	Is but a little way above our heads,
	Staying for thine to keep him company.
	Either thou or I, or both, must go with him. 125
TYBALT	Thou, wretched boy, that didst consort him here,
	Shalt with him hence!
ROMEO	(*Drawing his sword*) This shall determine that.

They fight. ROMEO *kills* TYBALT.

BENVOLIO	Romeo, away, be gone!
	The citizens are up, and Tybalt slain.
	Stand not amazed! The Prince will doom thee death 130
	If thou art taken. Hence, be gone, away!
ROMEO	O, I am fortune's fool!
BENVOLIO	Why dost thou stay?

Exit ROMEO.

Enter an OFFICER, *and armed citizens.*

OFFICER	Which way ran he that killed Mercutio?
	Tybalt, that murderer, which way ran he?
BENVOLIO	There lies that Tybalt.
OFFICER	Up, sir, go with me. 135
	I charge thee in the Prince's name, obey.

Enter PRINCE ESCALUS, MONTAGUE *and* CAPULET, *their* LADIES,
servants and attendants.

PRINCE	Where are the vile beginners of this fray?

Lady Capulet calls upon the
Prince to punish the Montagues
for Tybalt's death. Benvolio
reports how Mercutio and Tybalt
came to be killed.

Think about

- What differences do you
  notice between Benvolio's
  account of the fight (lines
  148 to 171) and what
  actually happened? Is his
  version of the story biased
  in favour of the Montagues
  as Lady Capulet claims?

138 **discover**: reveal
139 **manage**: sequence of events

144 **true**: fair and just

149 **spoke him fair**: spoke politely to him
    bid him bethink: asked him to consider
150 **nice**: trivial
    urged withal: also stressed
153 **take truce with**: pacify / calm
    unruly spleen: uncontrolled temper
154 **tilts**: thrusts
156 **all as hot**: just as angry
157 **martial scorn**: aggressive contempt

159 **dexterity**: skill
160 **Retorts it**: turns it back

163 **'twixt**: between
164 **envious**: intending harm
165 **stout**: brave
166 **by and by**: almost at once
167 **but newly entertained**: just at that
    moment thought about

173 **Affection ... false**: i.e. he is lying
    because he is a Montague
174 **black strife**: fatal conflict

BENVOLIO	O noble Prince, I can discover all
	The unlucky manage of this fatal brawl.
	There lies the man, slain by young Romeo, **140**
	That slew thy kinsman, brave Mercutio.
LADY CAPULET	Tybalt, my cousin? O, my brother's child!
	O Prince! O husband! O, the blood is spilled
	Of my dear kinsman! Prince, as thou art true,
	For blood of ours, shed blood of Montague! **145**
	O cousin, cousin!
PRINCE	Benvolio, who began this bloody fray?
BENVOLIO	Tybalt, here slain, whom Romeo's hand did slay.
	Romeo, that spoke him fair, bid him bethink
	How nice the quarrel was, and urged withal **150**
	Your high displeasure. All this, utterèd
	With gentle breath, calm look, knees humbly bowed,
	Could not take truce with the unruly spleen
	Of Tybalt, deaf to peace, but that he tilts
	With piercing steel at bold Mercutio's breast – **155**
	Who, all as hot, turns deadly point to point,
	And, with a martial scorn, with one hand beats
	Cold death aside, and with the other sends
	It back to Tybalt, whose dexterity
	Retorts it. Romeo he cries aloud, **160**
	'Hold, friends! Friends part!' – and, swifter than his
	tongue,
	His agile arm beats down their fatal points,
	And 'twixt them rushes, underneath whose arm
	An envious thrust from Tybalt hit the life
	Of stout Mercutio, and then Tybalt fled – **165**
	But by and by comes back to Romeo,
	Who had but newly entertained revenge,
	And to 't they go like lightning: for, ere I
	Could draw to part them, was stout Tybalt slain,
	And as he fell did Romeo turn and fly. **170**
	This is the truth, or let Benvolio die.
LADY CAPULET	He is a kinsman to the Montague.
	Affection makes him false! He speaks not true.
	Some twenty of them fought in this black strife,

Lady Capulet demands Romeo's death. Instead the Prince banishes Romeo from Verona.

179 **Who ... owe**: Who is now to pay for shedding Mercutio's precious blood

181 **His fault ... end**: His crime has simply put into effect what the law would have demanded

183 **exile**: banish (from Verona)

184 **have an interest**: am personally concerned

185 **My blood**: i.e. Mercutio, his kinsman

186 **amerce**: punish

189 **purchase out abuses**: buy a pardon for crimes

190 **Let Romeo hence**: Romeo must leave here

192 **attend our will**: come with me to hear what I intend to do

193 **Mercy ... kill**: Mercy will only cause more murders, if killers are pardoned

Think about

• In Act 1 Scene 1 the Prince said that death would be the penalty for any future fighting. How fair is his punishment of Romeo here, in your opinion? How effective is it likely to be in ending the feud? How good a ruler does it show him to be?

• Which statements are made at the end of this scene by Lady Capulet and by Montague that suggest that the feud will continue?

	And all those twenty could but kill one life.	175
	I beg for justice, which thou, Prince, must give:	
	Romeo slew Tybalt. Romeo must not live.	
PRINCE	Romeo slew him; *he* slew Mercutio.	
	Who now the price of his dear blood doth owe?	
MONTAGUE	Not Romeo, Prince – he was Mercutio's friend.	180
	His fault concludes but what the law should end –	
	The life of Tybalt.	
PRINCE	And for that offence	
	Immediately we do exile him hence!	
	I have an interest in your hate's proceedings:	
	My blood for your rude brawls doth lie a-bleeding.	185
	But I'll amerce you with so strong a fine	
	That you shall all repent the loss of mine.	
	I will be deaf to pleading and excuses –	
	Nor tears, nor prayers shall purchase out abuses.	
	Therefore use none. Let Romeo hence in haste:	190
	Else, when he is found, that hour is his last.	
	Bear hence this body, and attend our will.	
	Mercy but murders, pardoning those that kill.	

Exeunt.

RSC, 1986

RSC, 2004

Haymarket Theatre, Basingstoke, 2001

Romeo and Juliet, 1996 (directed by B. Luhrmann)

In this scene ...

- Juliet is longing for night and Romeo's arrival, when the Nurse enters, grieving at Tybalt's death.
- When Juliet realises that Romeo killed Tybalt, her feelings are at first confused. Then it sinks in that Romeo is banished and she becomes desperate.
- The Nurse offers comfort, promising to bring Romeo to Juliet that night.

As Juliet is wishing for night and Romeo's arrival, the Nurse enters.

Think about

- What does Juliet's language tell us about her mood? Think about (a) her use of words to do with night; and (b) her use of commands, like 'Gallop' and 'Come'.

- Much of Juliet's language in this speech has a sexual meaning, some of which is open (e.g. 'true love acted' in line 16) and some which is hidden (e.g. 'die' in line 21). How important is sexual attraction in Romeo and Juliet's relationship?

1 **apace**: quickly
2 **Phoebus' lodging**: the sun-god's home (i.e. the West – where the sun sets)
   waggoner: chariot-driver
3 **Phaeton**: Phoebus's son, who drove the sun-god's chariot
5 **close**: concealing
   love-performing: when acts of love take place
6 **runaway's ... wink**: any night-wanderer may sleep
8 **amorous rites**: sacred acts of love
10 **civil**: respectable
12 **learn ... match**: teach me how to lose my virginity but win a husband
13 **a pair ... maidenhoods**: i.e. they will both lose their virginity
14 **Hood ... cheeks**: i.e. cover up my blushes
   unmanned: 1 untamed; 2 with no sexual experience of men
15 **black mantle**: dark covering of night
   strange: 1 new to me; 2 shy
16 **Think ... modesty**: will consider the physical act of love to be chastity
25 **garish**: crudely bright
26 **mansion**: house
28 **tedious**: long drawn-out

In the Capulet house.

Enter Juliet, *alone.*

JULIET	Gallop apace, you fiery-footed steeds,
	Towards Phoebus' lodging! Such a waggoner
	As Phaeton would whip you to the west,
	And bring in cloudy night immediately.
	Spread thy close curtain, love-performing night –

Gallop apace, you fiery-footed steeds,
Towards Phoebus' lodging! Such a waggoner
As Phaeton would whip you to the west,
And bring in cloudy night immediately.
Spread thy close curtain, love-performing night –   5
That runaway's eyes may wink, and Romeo
Leap to these arms untalked of and unseen!
Lovers can see to do their amorous rites
By their own beauties – or, if love be blind
It best agrees with night. Come, civil night,   10
Thou sober-suited matron all in black,
And learn me how to lose a winning match,
Played for a pair of stainless maidenhoods.
Hood my unmanned blood, bating in my cheeks,
With thy black mantle – till strange love, grown bold,   15
Think true love acted simple modesty.
Come night – come Romeo! Come, thou day in night –
For thou wilt lie upon the wings of night,
Whiter than new snow upon a raven's back.
Come, gentle night: come loving, black-browed night –   20
Give me my Romeo! And when I shall die,
Take him and cut him out in little stars –
And he will make the face of heaven so fine
That all the world will be in love with night
And pay no worship to the garish sun.   25
O, I have bought the mansion of a love,
But not possessed it – and though I am sold,
Not yet enjoyed. So tedious is this day
As is the night before some festival
To an impatient child that hath new robes   30
And may not wear them. O, here comes my Nurse –

Enter the Nurse, *with the rope-ladder.*

And she brings news – and every tongue that speaks

Seeing the Nurse's grief, Juliet is desperate, thinking at first that it is Romeo who has died.

33 **eloquence**: beautifully expressed language
34 **cords**: rope-ladder

38 **undone**: ruined

40 **envious**: intending harm / spiteful

45–50 **Ay**: 1 yes; 2 the pronoun 'I'; 3 'eye'
47 **cockatrice**: mythical creature whose look could kill
49 **those eyes shut**: i.e. Romeo's eyes closed in death
51 **determine ... woe**: will decide my happiness or misery
53 **God ... mark**: forgive me for saying something so awful
54 **corse**: corpse
55 **bedaubed**: spattered with
56 **gore**: clotted
   swounded: fainted
57 **bankrupt**: someone who has lost all their money and will be imprisoned for their debts
   break: become 'broke' (wordplay)
59 **Vile ... here**: Body, surrender to the grave and end activity
60 **And thou ... bier**: both my corpse and Romeo's lie on the same sad funeral carriage

Think about

• Why do you think the Nurse does not tell Juliet straight away that it is Tybalt who has died?

• Why might the Nurse refer to Tybalt as 'the best friend I had' (line 61)?

But Romeo's name, speaks heavenly eloquence.
Now, Nurse, what news? What hast thou there? The cords
That Romeo bid thee fetch?

NURSE	Ay, ay, the cords.	35

She drops the rope-ladder on the floor.

JULIET   Ay me, what news? Why dost thou wring thy hands?

NURSE   Ah, well-a-day! He's dead, he's dead, he's dead!
We are undone, lady, we are undone.
Alack the day! He's gone, he's killed, he's dead!

JULIET   Can heaven be so envious?

NURSE   Romeo can –   40
Though heaven cannot. O Romeo, Romeo!
Whoever would have thought it? Romeo!

JULIET   What devil art thou dost torment me thus?
This torture should be roared in dismal hell!
Hath Romeo slain himself? Say thou but 'Ay',   45
And that bare vowel 'I' shall poison more
Than the death-darting eye of cockatrice.
I am not I, if there be such an 'I',
Or those eyes shut that makes thee answer 'Ay'.
If he be slain, say 'Ay', or if not, 'No'.   50
Brief sounds determine of my weal or woe.

NURSE   I saw the wound, I saw it with mine eyes –
God save the mark! – here on his manly breast.
A piteous corse – a bloody, piteous corse,
Pale, pale as ashes! – All bedaubed in blood,   55
All in gore blood! I swounded at the sight!

JULIET   O break, my heart! Poor bankrupt, break at once!
To prison, eyes: ne'er look on liberty!
Vile earth, to earth resign, end motion here –
And thou and Romeo press one heavy bier!   60

NURSE   O Tybalt, Tybalt, the best friend I had!
O courteous Tybalt, honest gentleman,
That ever I should live to see thee dead!

When Juliet realises that Romeo has killed Tybalt, she bitterly accuses Romeo of hiding wickedness behind a beautiful appearance. But when the Nurse criticises Romeo, Juliet is angry and defends him.

64 **so contrary**: first in one direction, then in the other

67 **dreadful ... doom**: blow, trumpet, to signal Judgement Day

73 **serpent heart**: Romeo is compared with the serpent which tempted Eve in the Garden of Eden in the Bible.
    flowering: youthful and fair
74 **keep**: live in
76 **wolvish-ravening**: ravenous as a wolf
77 **Despisèd**: detested
    divinest: most holy
78 **Just**: exactly
81 **bower**: beautifully enclose

86–7 **All ... forsworn**: They all lie and break their promises
87 **naught**: sinful
    dissemblers: cheats / deceivers
88 **aqua-vitae**: strong drink (brandy)

---Think about---

• Which oxymorons (expressions that seem to contradict themselves while still making sense) best express the conflict between Juliet's anger at Romeo and her relief that he is alive?

95 **chide at**: speak harshly of

JULIET	What storm is this that blows so contrary?
	Is Romeo slaughtered, and is Tybalt dead? 65
	My dearest cousin *and* my dearer lord?
	Then, dreadful trumpet, sound the general doom! –
	For who is living if those two are gone?

NURSE	Tybalt is gone – and Romeo banishèd.
	Romeo that killed him – *he* is banishèd! 70

JULIET	O God! Did Romeo's hand shed Tybalt's blood?

NURSE	It did, it did! Alas the day, it did!

JULIET	O serpent heart, hid with a flowering face!
	Did ever dragon keep so fair a cave?
	Beautiful tyrant, fiend angelical! – 75
	Dove-feathered raven, wolvish-ravening lamb! –
	Despisèd substance of divinest show –
	Just opposite to what thou justly seem'st,
	A damnèd saint, an honourable villain!
	O nature, what hadst thou to do in hell 80
	When thou didst bower the spirit of a fiend
	In mortal paradise of such sweet flesh?
	Was ever book containing such vile matter
	So fairly bound? O, that deceit should dwell
	In such a gorgeous palace!

NURSE	There's no trust, 85
	No faith, no honesty in men. – All perjured,
	All forsworn, all naught, all dissemblers!
	Ah, where's my man? Give me some aqua-vitae.
	These griefs, these woes, these sorrows make me old.
	Shame come to Romeo!

JULIET	Blistered be thy tongue 90
	For such a wish! He was not born to shame!
	Upon his brow shame is ashamed to sit,
	For 'tis a throne where honour may be crowned
	Sole monarch of the universal earth.
	O, what a beast was I to chide at him! 95

NURSE	Will you speak well of him that killed your cousin?

Confused by what has happened, Juliet tries to sort out her true feelings. She becomes desperate as it gradually sinks in that Romeo has been banished from Verona.

98 smooth thy name: speak well of you

100 wherefore: why

102 native spring: source
103 tributary drops: i.e. tears
104 mistaking: having made a mistake

109 fain: gladly

114 Hath slain: i.e. is as bad as the deaths of
116 delights in fellowship: likes company
117 needly … ranked: has to be included

120 modern … moved: might have caused an ordinary kind of grief
121 rear-ward: rearguard (i.e. following up behind)

125 bound: limit
126 sound: 1 give expression to; 2 measure the depth of

128 corse: corpse

130 spent: shed

132 beguiled: cheated

Think about

• Actor Niamh Cusack said 'this scene is where Juliet really grows up: she understands what commitment and depth of love are.' What does Juliet say here which supports this view?

JULIET	Shall I speak ill of him that is my husband?
	Ah, poor my lord, what tongue shall smooth thy name,
	When I, thy three-hours' wife, have mangled it?
	But wherefore, villain, didst thou kill my cousin?

JULIET   Shall I speak ill of him that is my husband?
            Ah, poor my lord, what tongue shall smooth thy name,
            When I, thy three-hours' wife, have mangled it?
            But wherefore, villain, didst thou kill my cousin?   100
            That villain cousin would have killed my husband.
            Back, foolish tears, back to your native spring –
            Your tributary drops belong to woe,
            Which you, mistaking, offer up to joy.
            My husband lives, that Tybalt would have slain,   105
            And Tybalt's dead that would have slain my husband.
            All this is comfort. Wherefore weep I then?
            Some word there was, worser than Tybalt's death,
            That murdered me. I would forget it fain,
            But O, it presses to my memory   110
            Like damnèd guilty deeds to sinners' minds:
            'Tybalt is dead, and Romeo banishèd.'
            That 'banishèd', that one word 'banishèd',
            Hath slain ten thousand Tybalts! Tybalt's death
            Was woe enough if it had ended there –   115
            Or, if sour woe delights in fellowship
            And needly will be ranked with other griefs,
            Why followed not, when she said, 'Tybalt's dead',
            'Thy father', or 'thy mother', nay, or both,
            Which modern lamentation might have moved?   120
            But with a rear-ward following Tybalt's death,
            'Romeo is banishèd'! To speak that word
            Is father, mother, Tybalt, Romeo, Juliet –
            All slain, all dead! 'Romeo is banishèd'.
            There is no end, no limit, measure, bound,   125
            In that word's death. No words can that woe sound.
            Where is my father and my mother, Nurse?

NURSE   Weeping and wailing over Tybalt's corse.
            Will you go to them? I will bring you thither.

JULIET   Wash they his wounds with tears? Mine shall be spent   130
            When theirs are dry, for Romeo's banishment.
            Take up those cords. Poor ropes, you are beguiled,
            Both you and I, for Romeo is exiled.
            He made you for a highway to my bed,

The Nurse knows that Romeo is hiding at the Friar's cell. She promises to bring him to Juliet.

137 **maidenhead**: virginity

138 **Hie**: Hurry

139 **wot**: know

Think about

- Juliet experiences some dramatic changes of emotion in this scene. Look at the following lines and decide what feelings she might be experiencing at each point: 1, 31, 36, 43, 57, 64, 71, 73, 90, 100 to 101, 106, 112 to 113, and 142 to 143.

	But I, a maid, die maiden-widowèd.	**135**
	Come cords – come Nurse. I'll to my wedding-bed –	
	And death, not Romeo, take my maidenhead!	

NURSE (*Gathering up the rope-ladder*) Hie to your chamber.
        I'll find Romeo
To comfort you. I wot well where he is.
Hark ye, your Romeo will be here at night: **140**
I'll to him – he is hid at Lawrence' cell.

JULIET O, find him! Give this ring to my true knight,
And bid him come to take his last farewell.

Exeunt.

In this scene ...

- Romeo is desperate when he hears that he has been banished from Verona, and the Friar cannot comfort him.
- The Nurse arrives. Fearing that Juliet must now hate him and imagining her grief, Romeo threatens to kill himself, but is prevented by the Friar and the Nurse.
- The Friar instructs Romeo to leave for Mantua by dawn at the latest, after he has spent the night with Juliet.

The Friar tells Romeo the Prince's sentence: that he is banished from Verona. He is angry with Romeo for not being grateful to have avoided a death sentence.

1 **fearful**: frightened
2 **Affliction ... parts**: You seem to be attracting suffering
3 **calamity**: great misfortune
4 **doom**: judgement / sentence
5 **craves ... hand**: wants to be introduced to me
6–7 **Too ... company**: i.e. You already know it too well

9 **doomsday**: Judgement Day (i.e. death)

10 **vanished from**: came out of

17 **without**: outside
18 **purgatory**: where souls had to wait and suffer for their sins before being allowed into heaven
20 **world's exile**: exile from the world
21 **mis-termed**: given the wrong name

24 **deadly**: that will lead to damnation
25 **Thy fault ... death**: Your crime is punishable by death
26 **rushed**: pushed
28 **dear**: unusual and precious

Think about

- Given that Romeo expected the death sentence (line 9), why does he react so badly to the news that he is to be banished? How sympathetic are you to his reactions here?

Friar Lawrence's cell.

Enter FRIAR LAWRENCE.

FR. LAWRENCE	Romeo, come forth! Come forth, thou fearful man.
	Affliction is enamoured of thy parts,
	And thou art wedded to calamity.

Enter ROMEO, *from an inner room.*

ROMEO	Father, what news? What is the Prince's doom?	
	What sorrow craves acquaintance at my hand	5
	That I yet know not?	
FR. LAWRENCE	Too familiar	
	Is my dear son with such sour company!	
	I bring thee tidings of the Prince's doom.	
ROMEO	What less than doomsday is the Prince's doom?	
FR. LAWRENCE	A gentler judgement vanished from his lips:	10
	Not body's death, but body's banishment.	
ROMEO	Ha! Banishment? Be merciful – say 'death' –	
	For exile hath more terror in his look,	
	Much more than death. Do not say 'banishment'!	
FR. LAWRENCE	Hence from Verona art thou banishèd.	15
	Be patient, for the world is broad and wide.	
ROMEO	There is no world without Verona walls,	
	But purgatory, torture, hell itself!	
	Hence 'banishèd' is banished from the world,	
	And world's exile is death. Then 'banishèd'	20
	Is death mis-termed. Calling death 'banishèd',	
	Thou cut'st my head off with a golden axe,	
	And smilest upon the stroke that murders me!	
FR. LAWRENCE	O deadly sin! O rude unthankfulness!	
	Thy fault our law calls death. But the kind Prince,	25
	Taking thy part, hath rushed aside the law,	
	And turned that black word 'death' to 'banishment'.	
	This is dear mercy, and thou seest it not.	

Romeo is devastated because banishment means that he will be separated from Juliet. He refuses to listen to the Friar's words of comfort.

Think about

• How does Romeo's language convey his insistence on seeing the worst of his situation and his refusal to accept the Friar's words of consolation? Look, for example, at the repeated words and language he uses to convey the unfairness of being removed from Juliet.

33 **validity**: value
34 **courtship**: 1 courtly behaviour; 2 opportunity for wooing
35 **carrion flies**: flies which live off rotting flesh
38 **vestal**: virginal

43 **say'st thou yet**: do you still say

45 **mean**: means
     though … mean: however dishonourable
48 **attends**: accompanies
49 **divine**: holy man
     ghostly: spiritual
50 **my friend professed**: someone who claims to be my friend
51 **mangle**: destroy
52 **fond**: foolish

55 **Adversity**: misfortune
     philosophy: the ability to understand and accept what happens

59 **Displant**: transplant / move to another place
60 **prevails not**: is of no effect / is no use

63 **dispute … estate**: discuss your situation with you

ROMEO	'Tis torture and not mercy. Heaven is here	
	Where Juliet lives! – and every cat and dog	30
	And little mouse, every unworthy thing,	
	Live here in heaven and may look on her,	
	But Romeo may not. More validity,	
	More honourable state, more courtship, lives	
	In carrion flies than Romeo: they may seize	35
	On the white wonder of dear Juliet's hand,	
	And steal immortal blessing from her lips,	
	Who even in pure and vestal modesty	
	Still blush, as thinking their own kisses sin.	
	But Romeo may not: he is banishèd!	40
	Flies may do this, but I from this must fly:	
	They are free men, but I am banishèd.	
	And say'st thou yet that exile is not death?	
	Hadst thou no poison mixed, no sharp-ground knife,	
	No sudden mean of death, though ne'er so mean,	45
	But 'banishèd' to kill me? 'Banishèd'!	
	O Friar, the damnèd use that word in hell.	
	Howling attends it! How hast thou the heart,	
	Being a divine, a ghostly confessor,	
	A sin-absolver, and my friend professed,	50
	To mangle me with that word 'banishèd'?	

| FR. LAWRENCE | Thou fond mad man! – Hear me a little speak. | |

| ROMEO | O, thou wilt speak again of banishment. | |

FR. LAWRENCE	I'll give thee armour to keep off that word –	
	Adversity's sweet milk, philosophy,	55
	To comfort thee though thou art banishèd.	

ROMEO	Yet 'banishèd'? Hang up philosophy!	
	Unless philosophy can make a Juliet,	
	Displant a town, reverse a Prince's doom,	
	It helps not, it prevails not! Talk no more.	60

| FR. LAWRENCE | O, then I see that madmen have no ears. | |

| ROMEO | How should they, when that wise men have no eyes? | |

| FR. LAWRENCE | Let me dispute with thee of thy estate. | |

Romeo is overcome with
emotion and flings himself to
the floor. He refuses to move,
even when someone knocks at
the door. It is the Nurse.

67 **Doting**: being deeply in love

70 **Taking ... of**: measuring out / taking
the space of

73 **infold**: wrap me up and hide me

75 **taken**: caught / arrested
Stay: Wait
76 **By and by**: I'll be with you straight
away
77 **simpleness**: foolishness

Think about

• How does the way Romeo
reacts to the word
'banishèd' here (line 67),
compare with Juliet's
reaction to the word in Act 3
Scene 2?

• If you were the director,
how would you stage lines
70 to 88? Think about
(a) how the characters are
feeling and what their
reactions will be; (b) where
they should be positioned
on stage; and (c) when and
how the characters should
move.

84 **even ... case**: in exactly the same state
as my mistress ('case' could also
sometimes mean pregnancy)
85 **woeful sympathy**: they're feeling the
same grief

ROMEO	Thou canst not speak of that thou dost not feel!
	Wert thou as young as I, Juliet thy love, 65
	An hour but married, Tybalt murderèd,
	Doting like me, and like me banishèd,
	Then mightst thou speak! – then mightst thou tear thy hair,
	And fall upon the ground as I do now,
	Taking the measure of an unmade grave! 70

He flings himself down on the floor. A knocking is heard.

FR. LAWRENCE	Arise! One knocks. Good Romeo, hide thyself.
ROMEO	Not I – unless the breath of heartsick groans
	Mist-like infold me from the search of eyes.

More knocking heard.

FR. LAWRENCE	Hark how they knock! – (*Calling*) Who's there? – Romeo, arise!
	Thou wilt be taken. – (*Calling*) Stay a while! – Stand up! 75
	Run to my study. – (*Calling*) By and by! – God's will! –
	What simpleness is this? – (*Calling*) I come, I come!

Louder knocking from the door.

	Who knocks so hard? Whence come you? What's your will?
NURSE	(*Calling from outside*) Let me come in and you shall know my errand!
	I come from Lady Juliet.
FR. LAWRENCE	(*Opening the door*) Welcome then. 80
NURSE	(*Entering*) O holy Friar – O tell me, holy Friar,
	Where's my lady's lord? Where's Romeo?
FR. LAWRENCE	There on the ground, with his own tears made drunk.
NURSE	O, he is even in my mistress' case,
	Just in her case! O woeful sympathy! 85
	Piteous predicament! Even so lies she,
	Blubbering and weeping, weeping and blubbering.
	Stand up, stand up! Stand, and you be a man!

Romeo fears that Juliet must now hate him for having killed her cousin, Tybalt. He draws a dagger to kill himself, but the Friar prevents him, furious at Romeo's behaviour.

89 **rise and stand**: both words can also mean 'have an erection'

90 **an O**: 1 a fit of groaning; 2 the vagina

93 **old**: hardened / great

95 **removed but little**: closely related (Tybalt was Juliet's cousin)

97 **concealed**: i.e. she is secretly his wife

99 **now**: one minute

102 **level**: aim

105 **anatomy**: body

106 **sack**: destroy

Think about

- The Nurse's language (lines 84 to 90) includes several examples of sexual innuendo (double-meanings). Does she intend them? What effect do they have on an audience here (a) if she intends them; and (b) if she does not realise what she is saying?

- What seems to be the Nurse's intentions in the way she deals with Romeo and describes Juliet's behaviour to him?

108 **form**: physical shape

109 **denote**: are the sign of

110 **unreasonable**: lacking human reason

111 **Unseemly**: behaving inappropriately

112 **ill-beseeming**: unnatural and wrong

114 **disposition**: personality / character
     better tempered: was more stable

117 **damnèd hate**: i.e. suicide

118 **rail'st thou on**: curse

121 **shape**: (manly) physical appearance
     wit: intellect

| | For Juliet's sake – for her sake rise and stand! | |
| | Why should you fall into so deep an O? | 90 |

ROMEO   (*Getting up*) Nurse!

NURSE   Ah, sir! Ah, sir! Death's the end of all.

ROMEO   Spak'st thou of Juliet? How is it with her?
            Doth she not think me an old murderer,
            Now I have stained the childhood of our joy
            With blood removed but little from her own?   95
            Where is she? And how doth she? And what says
            My concealed lady to our cancelled love?

NURSE   O, she says nothing, sir – but weeps and weeps,
            And now falls on her bed, and then starts up,
            And Tybalt calls, and then on Romeo cries,   100
            And then down falls again!

ROMEO   As if that name,
            Shot from the deadly level of a gun,
            Did murder her, as that name's cursèd hand
            Murdered her kinsman. O, tell me, Friar, tell me,
            In what vile part of this anatomy   105
            Doth my name lodge? Tell me! – that I may sack
            The hateful mansion!

He draws his dagger as if to stab himself.

FR. LAWRENCE   Hold thy desperate hand!
            Art thou a man? Thy form cries out thou art:
            Thy tears are womanish – thy wild acts denote
            The unreasonable fury of a beast!   110
            Unseemly woman in a seeming man,
            And ill-beseeming beast in seeming both!
            Thou hast amazed me! By my holy order,
            I thought thy disposition better tempered.
            Hast thou slain Tybalt? Wilt thou slay thyself?   115
            And slay thy lady, that in thy life lives,
            By doing damnèd hate upon thyself?
            Why rail'st thou on thy birth, the heaven, and earth,
            Since birth, and heaven, and earth, all three, do meet
            In thee at once, which thou at once wouldst lose? 120
            Fie, fie! Thou sham'st thy shape, thy love, thy wit,

The Friar tells Romeo to count his blessings and instructs him to visit Juliet as planned, but to leave for Mantua by dawn at the latest. The Friar will try to find an opportunity to explain to everyone in Verona what has happened.

122   **usurer**: money-lender
      abound'st: are wealthy
123   **usest ... use**: do not spend your wealth properly
124   **bedeck**: be an ornament to
125   **form of wax**: i.e. poor copy
126   **Digressing**: deviating
127   **hollow perjury**: empty lies
130   **Misshapen ... both**: leading both (i.e. manliness and love) astray
131   **powder**: gunpowder
      skilless: i.e. careless
133   **dismembered**: blown limb from limb
      with ... defence: by the very thing that should protect you
135   **but lately dead**: only a few minutes ago as good as dead
136   **There ... happy**: in that you are fortunate
140   **light**: alight / land
141   **best array**: finest clothes
145   **decreed**: arranged
147   **look ... set**: take care you don't stay until the night-patrol goes on duty
148   **pass**: get through the city gates
      Mantua: the nearest city to Verona

150   **blaze**: make publicly known
      reconcile your friends: bring your two families together
153   **lamentation**: grieving

156   **heavy ... unto**: grief over Tybalt will make them ready for

159   **counsel**: advice

166

Which like a usurer abound'st in all,
And usest none in that true use indeed
Which should bedeck thy shape, thy love, thy wit.
Thy noble shape is but a form of wax,   125
Digressing from the valour of a man –
Thy dear love sworn but hollow perjury,
Killing that love which thou hast vowed to cherish!
Thy wit, that ornament to shape and love,
Misshapen in the conduct of them both,   130
Like powder in a skilless soldier's flask,
Is set afire by thine own ignorance,
And thou dismembered with thine own defence.
What? Rouse thee, man! Thy Juliet is alive,
For whose dear sake thou wast but lately dead: 135
There art thou happy. Tybalt would kill thee,
But thou slew'st Tybalt. There art thou happy.
The law that threatened death becomes thy friend,
And turns it to exile. There art thou happy too.
A pack of blessings light upon thy back;   140
Happiness courts thee in her best array –
But like a misbehaved and sullen wench
Thou frown'st upon thy fortune and thy love.
Take heed, take heed! – for such die miserable.
Go – get thee to thy love, as was decreed.   145
Ascend her chamber: hence, and comfort her –
But look thou stay not till the watch be set,
For then thou canst not pass to Mantua,
Where thou shalt live till we can find a time
To blaze your marriage, reconcile your friends,   150
Beg pardon of the Prince, and call thee back
With twenty hundred thousand times more joy
Than thou went'st forth in lamentation.
Go before, Nurse. Commend me to thy lady,
And bid her hasten all the house to bed –   155
Which heavy sorrow makes them apt unto.
Romeo is coming.

NURSE   O Lord, I could have stayed here all the night
To hear good counsel! O, what learning is!
My lord, I'll tell my lady you will come.   160

Romeo is comforted when the Nurse gives him Juliet's ring. The Friar promises to send messages to Romeo in Mantua, and Romeo goes to meet Juliet.

161 **chide**: rebuke me / tell me off

164 **comfort**: happiness

165 **here ... state**: your future happiness depends on this (i.e. on following my instructions)

168 **Sojourn**: Stay for the time being

169 **signify**: report

170 **good hap**: fortunate thing
     chances: happens

172 **But ... me**: Were it not that I am called away by the greatest of joys (i.e. of being with Juliet)

173 **It were ... thee**: I would be very sad to leave you in such a hurry

---Think about ---------

• Romeo's mood seems to change strikingly at the end of this scene. What causes him to cheer up? What does this mood-swing suggest about him?

ROMEO	Do so, and bid my sweet prepare to chide.
NURSE	(*Leaving, but turning back again to* ROMEO) Here, sir – a ring she bid me give you, sir. Hie you, make haste – for it grows very late.

Exit.

ROMEO	How well my comfort is revived by this.

FR. LAWRENCE Go hence – good night – and here stands all your state: **165**
Either be gone before the watch be set,
Or by the break of day disguised from hence.
Sojourn in Mantua. I'll find out your man,
And he shall signify from time to time
Every good hap to you that chances here.   **170**
Give me thy hand. 'Tis late. Farewell, good night.

ROMEO	But that a joy past joy calls out on me, It were a grief so brief to part with thee. Farewell.

Exeunt.

Act 3   Scene 4

In this scene ...

- Capulet arranges with Paris that his wedding to Juliet will take place in a few days' time.
- He sends Lady Capulet to inform Juliet.

Capulet explains to Paris that Juliet cannot see him as she is mourning the death of her cousin, Tybalt. But he then tells Paris that he can marry Juliet the following Thursday.

1 **fallen out**: happened
2 **move**: persuade (i.e. to marry Paris)
3 **Look you**: You have to understand that

8 **afford**: allow
9 **Commend me**: Give my regards
10 **mind**: views (i.e. about the marriage)

11 **mewed ... heaviness**: shut away with sadness

12 **desperate tender**: bold offer

16 **son**: i.e. Capulet already sees Paris as a son-in-law
18 **soft**: wait a minute

Think about

- Do you have any sympathy for Paris and the situation he is in? Has he behaved badly either in this scene or in Act 1 Scene 2, in your opinion?

- How far do you blame him for being an obstacle in the way of Romeo and Juliet's happiness?

20 **O'**: On

23 **keep ... ado**: won't make a great fuss
24 **late**: recently
25 **held him carelessly**: did not care much about him
26 **kinsman**: relative
   revel much: have a big celebration

The Capulet house.

Enter CAPULET, LADY CAPULET, *and Count* PARIS.

CAPULET	Things have fallen out, sir, so unluckily
	That we have had no time to move our daughter.
	Look you, she loved her kinsman Tybalt dearly,
	And so did I. Well, we were born to die.
	'Tis very late. She'll not come down tonight. 5
	I promise you, but for your company,
	I would have been a-bed an hour ago.
PARIS	These times of woe afford no time to woo.
	Madam, good night. Commend me to your daughter.
LADY CAPULET	I will, and know her mind early tomorrow. 10
	Tonight she's mewed up to her heaviness.

PARIS *goes, but* CAPULET *calls him back.*

CAPULET	Sir Paris! – I will make a desperate tender
	Of my child's love. I think she will be ruled
	In all respects by me – nay more, I doubt it not.
	Wife, go you to her ere you go to bed. 15
	Acquaint her here of my son Paris' love,
	And bid her – mark you me? – on Wednesday next –
	But soft, what day is this?
PARIS	Monday, my lord.
CAPULET	Monday, ah ha! Well, Wednesday is too soon.
	O' Thursday let it be. O' Thursday, tell her, 20
	She shall be married to this noble earl.
	Will you be ready? Do you like this haste?
	We'll keep no great ado – a friend or two.
	For hark you, Tybalt being slain so late,
	It may be thought we held him carelessly, 25
	Being our kinsman, if we revel much.
	Therefore we'll have some half a dozen friends,
	And there an end. (*To* PARIS) But what say you to
	Thursday?

Capulet instructs his wife to tell Juliet of the wedding plans, and goes to bed.

29 **would**: wish

32 **against**: for

34 **Afore me**: My goodness
35 **by and by**: almost immediately

Think about

• What does this short scene tell us about Capulet as a father? Think about how concerned he is for his daughter's happiness and whether he understands her feelings. Look back at what he says in Act 1 Scene 2, lines 8 to 19, for example.

• What do you think about Lady Capulet's silence throughout this scene? How would you direct the actor to play her here?

PARIS	My lord, I would that Thursday were tomorrow!
CAPULET	Well, get you gone. O' Thursday be it then. 30

(To LADY CAPULET*)* Go you to Juliet ere you go to bed.
Prepare her, wife, against this wedding day.
Farewell, my lord. *(Calling for a servant)* Light to my
    chamber, ho!
Afore me! – 'tis so very late that we
May call it early by and by. Good night.   35

Exeunt.

ACT 3 SCENE 5

In this scene ...

- Having spent the night with Juliet, Romeo leaves for Mantua.
- Lady Capulet tells Juliet that she is to marry Paris, but she refuses.
- Capulet is furious with Juliet for her disobedience and threatens her.
- The Nurse advises Juliet to marry Paris. Juliet pretends to accept her advice, but privately plans to seek help from the Friar.

As their night together comes to an end, Juliet at first tries to persuade Romeo to stay longer. But she then fears for his safety and reluctantly encourages him to go.

2 **nightingale ... lark**: Nightingales are heard singing at night; larks begin at dawn.

7 **envious**: harmfully jealous
8 **severing**: parting
9 **Night's candles**: i.e. the stars
   jocund: cheerful

13 **exhales**: breathes out

17 **ta'en**: arrested
18 **so thou ... so**: so long as that is what you want
20 **reflex ... brow**: reflection of the moon's face (Cynthia was another name for Diana, the moon goddess.)
22 **vaulty**: arched
23 **care**: concern / desire

Think about

- According to the opening stage direction here, where might this scene have taken place in Shakespeare's theatre? If you were staging it or filming it today, where would you place the two lovers?

28 **sharps**: sharp notes
29 **division**: 1 melody; 2 separation (of the lovers)
31 **change**: exchanged (In folk-lore, the lark has dull eyes, and the toad remarkable ones.)

The Capulet garden, and Juliet's window-balcony.

Enter ROMEO *and* JULIET *above, at the window.*

JULIET
Wilt thou be gone? It is not yet near day.
It was the nightingale, and not the lark,
That pierced the fearful hollow of thine ear.
Nightly she sings on yond pomegranate tree.
Believe me, love, it was the nightingale.   5

ROMEO
It was the lark, the herald of the morn –
No nightingale. Look, love, what envious streaks
Do lace the severing clouds in yonder east.
Night's candles are burnt out, and jocund day
Stands tiptoe on the misty mountain tops.   10
I must be gone and live, or stay and die.

JULIET
Yond light is not daylight – I know it, I.
It is some meteor that the sun exhales
To be to thee this night a torch-bearer
And light thee on thy way to Mantua.   15
Therefore stay yet. Thou need'st not to be gone.

ROMEO
Let me be ta'en, let me be put to death –
I am content, so thou wilt have it so.
I'll say yon grey is not the morning's eye –
'Tis but the pale reflex of Cynthia's brow;   20
Nor that is not the lark whose notes do beat
The vaulty heaven so high above our heads.
I have more care to stay than will to go.
Come, death, and welcome! – Juliet wills it so.
How is't, my soul? Let's talk – it is not day.   25

JULIET
It is, it is! Hie hence, be gone! Away!
It is the lark that sings so out of tune,
Straining harsh discords and unpleasing sharps.
Some say the lark makes sweet division:
This doth not so, for she divideth us.   30
Some say the lark and loathèd toad change eyes.
O, now I would they had changed voices too! –

When the Nurse tells Juliet that
Lady Capulet is on her way,
Romeo climbs down the ladder.
As they part, Juliet experiences
a sense that something bad will
happen.

33 **arm from ... affray**: the lark's song
frightens us out of each other's arms
34 **hunt's-up**: a song to waken hunters

40 **wary**: careful

43 **ay**: for ever
friend: lover

46 **count**: method of counting
much in years: very old

52 **discourses**: conversations
53 **ill-divining**: prophesying bad things

---**Think about**---

• Both Romeo and Juliet
  describe their situation
  using strong images. What
  pictures form in your mind
  at line 36, and at lines 54
  to 55?

58 **Dry**: Thirsty (It was believed that
sorrow exhausted the blood.)

Since arm from arm that voice doth us affray,
Hunting thee hence with hunt's-up to the day.
O now be gone! – more light and light it grows.   35

ROMEO   More light and light, more dark and dark our woes.

Enter the NURSE, *hurriedly.*

NURSE   Madam!

JULIET   Nurse?

NURSE   Your lady mother is coming to your chamber!
The day is broke. Be wary, look about!   40

Exit NURSE.

JULIET   Then, window, let day in, and let life out.

ROMEO   Farewell, farewell. One kiss and I'll descend.

He goes down the rope-ladder, to the garden.

JULIET   Art thou gone so, love? – lord, ay husband, friend!
I must hear from thee every day in the hour,
For in a minute there are many days.   45
O, by this count I shall be much in years
Ere I again behold my Romeo!

ROMEO   (*From the garden below*) Farewell! I will omit no
        opportunity
That may convey my greetings, love, to thee.

JULIET   O, think'st thou we shall ever meet again?   50

ROMEO   I doubt it not. And all these woes shall serve
For sweet discourses in our time to come.

JULIET   O God, I have an ill-divining soul!
Methinks I see thee, now thou art so low,
As one dead in the bottom of a tomb.   55
Either my eyesight fails, or thou look'st pale.

ROMEO   And trust me, love, in my eye so do you.
Dry sorrow drinks our blood. Adieu, adieu!

Exit ROMEO.

Lady Capulet believes that Juliet is still weeping for Tybalt's death, and says how angry she is that his killer, Romeo, is still alive.

59 **fickle**: changeable
60 **what dost thou**: what business have you

65 **Is she … late**: Has she not yet gone to bed
66 **procures**: brings

67 **how now**: what's the matter

71 **Some**: A moderate amount of
72 **still**: always
    want of wit: lack of common sense
73 **feeling**: deeply felt

76 **friend**: can mean 'lover' (Juliet's private meaning)

80 **asunder**: apart

82 **like**: so much as

Think about

• If you were performing this play in Shakespeare's Globe Theatre, how would you stage the opening of this scene (up to Lady Capulet's entrance at line 67)? Think about the positions of characters on the stage, furniture, and entrances and exits, for example.

JULIET *pulls up the rope-ladder.*

JULIET	O, Fortune, Fortune! All men call thee fickle.
	If thou art fickle, what dost thou with him **60**
	That is renowned for faith? *Be* fickle, Fortune –
	For then I hope thou wilt not keep him long,
	But send him back.

LADY CAPULET (*From inside the house*) Ho, daughter, are you up?

JULIET   Who is't that calls? It is my lady mother.
                Is she not down so late, or up so early?   **65**
                What unaccustomed cause procures her hither?

Enter LADY CAPULET, *below.* JULIET *comes down from her*
window and enters to meet her mother.

LADY CAPULET   Why, how now, Juliet?

JULIET   Madam, I am not well.

LADY CAPULET   Evermore weeping for your cousin's death?
                What, wilt thou wash him from his grave with tears?
                And if thou couldst, thou couldst not make him live –   **70**
                Therefore have done. Some grief shows much of love,
                But much of grief shows still some want of wit.

JULIET   Yet let me weep for such a feeling loss.

LADY CAPULET   So shall you feel the loss, but not the friend
                Which you weep for.

JULIET   Feeling so the loss,   **75**
        I cannot choose but ever weep the friend.

LADY CAPULET   Well, girl, thou weep'st not so much for his death
                As that the villain lives which slaughtered him.

JULIET   What villain, madam?

LADY CAPULET   That same villain, Romeo.

JULIET   (*Aside*) Villain and he be many miles asunder. –   **80**
        (*To her mother*) God pardon him! I do, with all my
            heart –
        And yet no man like he doth grieve my heart.

LADY CAPULET   That is because the traitor murderer lives.

Lady Capulet promises that they will take revenge on Romeo by having him killed. But when she tells Juliet that she is to marry Paris on Thursday, Juliet forcefully refuses.

Think about

• Look at the exchange between Lady Capulet and Juliet (lines 67 to 101). For each of the following lines, decide (a) what Lady Capulet thinks Juliet means; and (b) what Juliet actually means: 67, 73, 75 to 76, 81, 82, 84, 85, 92 to 93, 95 to 98, 98 to 99, and 100 to 101.

• What do you think of the way Juliet replies in lines 115 to 122?

85 **venge**: get revenge for

88 **runagate**: fugitive villain
89 **unaccustomed dram**: strange dose (of poison)

94 **vexed**: angered

96 **temper**: 1 mix; 2 weaken / dilute

98 **abhors**: hates

100 **wreak the love**: 1 get revenge for my love (for Tybalt); 2 physically express my love (for Romeo)

104 **in such ... time**: when we most need it

106 **careful**: considerate / who wants the best for you
107 **heaviness**: sadness
108 **sorted out**: chosen
sudden: soon to come
109 **nor ... for**: and which I did not expect either
110 **in happy time**: it has come just at the right time

117 **wonder at**: am amazed at
118 **should be**: wants to be

JULIET	Ay, madam – from the reach of these my hands.
	Would none but I might venge my cousin's death! 85
LADY CAPULET	We will have vengeance for it, fear thou not.
	Then weep no more. I'll send to one in Mantua,
	Where that same banished runagate doth live,
	Shall give him such an unaccustomed dram
	That he shall soon keep Tybalt company – 90
	And then I hope thou wilt be satisfied.
JULIET	Indeed, I never shall be satisfied
	With Romeo till I behold him – dead –
	Is my poor heart, so for a kinsman vexed.
	Madam, if you could find out but a man 95
	To bear a poison, I would temper it
	That Romeo should upon receipt thereof
	Soon sleep in quiet. O, how my heart abhors
	To hear him named and cannot come to him –
	To wreak the love I bore my cousin 100
	Upon his body that hath slaughtered him!
LADY CAPULET	Find thou the means, and I'll find such a man.
	But now I'll tell thee joyful tidings, girl.
JULIET	And joy comes well in such a needy time.
	What are they, I beseech your ladyship? 105
LADY CAPULET	Well, well, thou hast a careful father, child –
	One who, to put thee from thy heaviness,
	Hath sorted out a sudden day of joy
	That thou expects not, nor I looked not for.
JULIET	Madam, in happy time! What day is that? 110
LADY CAPULET	Marry, my child, early next Thursday morn,
	The gallant, young, and noble gentleman,
	The County Paris, at Saint Peter's Church,
	Shall happily make thee there a joyful bride.
JULIET	Now, by Saint Peter's Church, and Peter too, 115
	He shall *not* make me there a joyful bride!
	I wonder at this haste, that I must wed
	Ere he that should be husband comes to woo!
	I pray you tell my lord and father, madam,

Capulet enters and finds Juliet in tears. He explodes with anger when he is told that Juliet is refusing to marry Paris.

124 **at your hands**: from you yourself

126 **sunset ... son**: i.e. Tybalt's death

128 **conduit**: street-fountain

130 **counterfeits**: are imitating
bark: ship
131 **still**: always / constantly

135 **Without**: unless there is
sudden calm: i.e. in the winds
overset: capsize
137 **decree**: decision

138 **will none**: refuses / will have none of it

140 **Soft ... you**: Wait a minute, I don't understand, say that again
142 **count her**: consider herself
143 **wrought**: arranged / secured
144 **bride**: bridegroom
147 **hate ... love**: a hateful action which was intended to be a loving one
148 **How ... chop-logic**: What do you mean, arguing like this
150 **minion**: spoilt brat
152 **fettle ... joints**: i.e. get yourself ready
'gainst: in preparation for
154 **hurdle**: wooden rack used for dragging criminals to their execution
155 **green-sickness carrion**: pale corpse
156 **tallow-face**: i.e. a face as white as candle-wax

Think about

- Capulet compares Juliet's mood to a ship at sea in stormy weather. Decide what particular comparisons he is making in the following lines, and how effective they are, in your opinion: 125 to 127, 128, 129, and 129 to 136.

- What do you think this language reveals about Capulet? Is he genuinely upset or is he selfishly thinking about his own interest in Juliet marrying Paris? Which of these interpretations would you choose to show on stage, if you were acting the part?

	I will not marry yet. And when I do, I swear	120
	It shall be Romeo, whom you know I hate,	
	Rather than Paris. These are news indeed!	

LADY CAPULET   Here comes your father. Tell him so yourself,
And see how he will take it at your hands.

Enter CAPULET, *and the* NURSE.

CAPULET   When the sun sets, the earth doth drizzle dew – 125
But for the sunset of my brother's son
It rains downright.
How now – a conduit, girl? What, still in tears?
Evermore showering? In one little body
Thou counterfeits a bark, a sea, a wind – 130
For still thy eyes, which I may call the sea,
Do ebb and flow with tears. The bark thy body is,
Sailing in this salt flood – the winds thy sighs,
Who raging with thy tears, and they with them,
Without a sudden calm will overset 135
Thy tempest-tossèd body. How now, wife?
Have you delivered to her our decree?

LADY CAPULET   Ay, sir – but she will none, she gives you thanks.
I would the fool were married to her grave!

CAPULET   Soft! – take me with you, take me with you, wife. 140
How will she none? Doth she not give us thanks?
Is she not proud? Doth she not count her blest,
Unworthy as she is, that we have wrought
So worthy a gentleman to be her bride?

JULIET   Not proud you have, but thankful that you have. 145
Proud can I never be of what I hate –
But thankful, even for hate that is meant love.

CAPULET   How, now! How, now – chop-logic? What is this?
'Proud', and 'I thank you', and 'I thank you not' –
And yet 'Not proud'? – mistress minion, you! 150
Thank me no thankings, nor proud me no prouds! –
But fettle your fine joints 'gainst Thursday next,
To go with Paris to Saint Peter's Church –
Or I will drag thee on a hurdle thither.
Out, you green-sickness carrion! Out, you baggage! 155
You tallow-face!

Maddened at Juliet's disobedience, Capulet threatens and insults her, ignoring the attempts by his wife and the Nurse to calm him down.

Think about

- In this scene Capulet abuses Juliet verbally (and, in some productions, physically too). What do you think he means by the insults in the following lines: 150, 155, 156, 159, 167, 183, and 184? How do you react to Capulet's violence?

- What features of Juliet's character and behaviour seem to be angering him most here?

156 **Fie**: For shame

163 **My fingers itch**: i.e. I'm tempted to hit you

167 **Out ... hilding**: Away with her, the worthless creature
168 **rate**: verbally attack

170 **Good Prudence**: Madam Wisdom
Smatter ... gossips: Natter with your women-friends
171 **God ... e'en**: i.e. for God's sake

173 **Utter ... bowl**: Save your serious words for when you're having a drink with your women-friends
174 **hot**: angry
175 **God's bread**: a powerful oath (referring to the bread used in the holy mass)
177 **still ... been**: the one thing I have always been concerned with
178 **have her matched**: provide a husband for her
180 **fair demesnes**: good estates
181 **parts**: qualities
182 **Proportioned ... man**: with as good a physique as you could hope for
183 **puling**: whimpering / whingeing
184 **whining mammet**: crying doll
in her fortune's tender: when good fortune is offered to her

184

LADY CAPULET	(*To her husband*) Fie, fie! What, are you mad?
JULIET	(*Kneeling*) Good father, I beseech you on my knees – Hear me with patience but to speak a word.
CAPULET	Hang thee, young baggage! Disobedient wretch! I tell thee what: get thee to church o' Thursday, Or never after look me in the face! Speak not, reply not, do not answer me! My fingers itch. Wife, we scarce thought us blest That God had lent us but this only child – But now I see this one is one too much, And that we have a curse in having her. Out on her, hilding!
NURSE	God in heaven bless her! You are to blame, my lord, to rate her so.
CAPULET	And why, my Lady Wisdom? Hold your tongue, Good Prudence! Smatter with your gossips. Go!
NURSE	I speak no treason.
CAPULET	O, God gi' good e'en!
NURSE	May not one speak?
CAPULET	Peace, you mumbling fool! Utter your gravity o'er a gossip's bowl, For here we need it not.
LADY CAPULET	You are too hot.
CAPULET	God's bread! It makes me mad! Day, night, hour, tide, time, work, play, Alone, in company – still my care hath been To have her matched! And having now provided A gentleman of noble parentage, Of fair demesnes, youthful and nobly trained, Stuffed, as they say, with honourable parts, Proportioned as one's thought would wish a man – And then to have a wretched puling fool, A whining mammet, in her fortune's tender, To answer 'I'll not wed. I cannot love. I am too young, I pray you pardon me'!

Line numbers in right margin: 160, 165, 170, 175, 180, 185

Capulet threatens to throw Juliet out of the house and to disown her unless she agrees to marry Paris. When her mother rejects her too, Juliet turns to the Nurse for comfort and advice.

187 **and**: if
188 **Graze**: Feed
house with me: live in my house
189 **do ... jest**: am not in the habit of making jokes
190 **Advise**: Give it some careful thought

194 **what ... good**: i.e. you will inherit none of my wealth
195 **be forsworn**: break my word

201 **monument**: tomb

205 **my ... heaven**: i.e. she has made marriage vows before God
206 **How ... earth**: How can I take my vows back
208 **By leaving earth**: i.e. by dying
209 **practise stratagems**: play deceitful tricks
210 **soft**: easy

213 **all ... nothing**: i.e. it's a perfectly safe bet
214 **challenge you**: claim you as his wife

219 **dishclout**: dishcloth
to: compared with
220 **green ... quick**: beautiful ... alive

Think about

• What does Lady Capulet reveal about herself in this scene? Look particularly at lines 67 to 102, 103 to 114, 123 to 124, 156, and 174. How far does she mean what she says in lines 139 and 203?

	But, and you will not wed, I'll pardon you!	
	Graze where you will – you shall not house with me!	
	Look to 't, think on't! I do not use to jest.	
	Thursday is near. Lay hand on heart. Advise.	**190**
	And you be mine, I'll give you to my friend:	
	And you be not, hang, beg, starve, die in the streets! –	
	For, by my soul, I'll ne'er acknowledge thee,	
	Nor what is mine shall never do thee good.	
	Trust to't, bethink you! I'll not be forsworn.	**195**

Exit.

JULIET	Is there no pity sitting in the clouds	
	That sees into the bottom of my grief?	
	O sweet my mother, cast me not away!	
	Delay this marriage for a month, a week –	
	Or, if you do not, make the bridal bed	**200**
	In that dim monument where Tybalt lies!	

LADY CAPULET	Talk not to me, for I'll not speak a word.
	Do as thou wilt, for I have done with thee.

Exit.

JULIET	O God! – O Nurse, how shall this be prevented?	
	My husband is on earth, my faith in heaven.	**205**
	How shall that faith return again to earth,	
	Unless that husband send it me from heaven	
	By leaving earth? Comfort me, counsel me.	
	Alack, alack, that heaven should practise stratagems	
	Upon so soft a subject as myself!	**210**
	What say'st thou? Hast thou not a word of joy?	
	Some comfort, Nurse?	

NURSE	Faith, here it is:	
	Romeo is banishèd – and all the world to nothing	
	That he dares ne'er come back to challenge you.	
	Or, if he do, it needs must be by stealth.	**215**
	Then, since the case so stands as now it doth,	
	I think it best you married with the County.	
	O, he's a lovely gentleman!	
	Romeo's a dishclout to him. An eagle, madam,	
	Hath not so green, so quick, so fair an eye	**220**

When the Nurse advises her to marry Paris, Juliet tells the Nurse to say that she has gone to Friar Lawrence for confession. In reality she goes, deperately, to seek the Friar's help.

221 **Beshrew**: Curse
222 **match**: marriage

224 **'twere ... were**: he might as well be
225 **here**: i.e. on earth / alive
    no use of him: without being able to enjoy him as a husband

228 **Amen**: So be it

233 **absolved**: forgiven for my sins

235 **Ancient damnation**: Damned old woman
236 **wish ... forsworn**: want me to break my marriage vows
237 **dispraise**: criticise / speak ill of
238 **with above compare**: as being beyond comparison
240 **bosom**: private thoughts
    twain: separated

Think about

• How might an actor playing Juliet say 'Amen' (line 228)?

• What is your opinion of the Nurse's advice (lines 212 to 225)?

• How do you feel about the Nurse by the end of this scene? Have your views about her changed?

	As Paris hath. Beshrew my very heart,	
	I think you are happy in this second match,	
	For it excels your first – or if it did not,	
	Your first is dead, or 'twere as good he were,	
	As living here, and you no use of him.	**225**
JULIET	Speak'st thou from thy heart?	
NURSE	And from my soul too – else beshrew them both.	
JULIET	Amen!	
NURSE	What?	
JULIET	Well, thou hast comforted me marvellous much.	**230**
	Go in, and tell my lady I am gone,	
	Having displeased my father, to Lawrence' cell –	
	To make confession and to be absolved.	
NURSE	Marry, I will; and this is wisely done.	

Exit.

JULIET	Ancient damnation! O most wicked fiend!	**235**
	Is it more sin to wish me thus forsworn,	
	Or to dispraise my lord with that same tongue	
	Which she hath praised him with above compare	
	So many thousand times? Go, counsellor! –	
	Thou and my bosom henceforth shall be twain.	**240**
	I'll to the Friar, to know his remedy.	
	If all else fail, myself have power to die.	

Exit.

Düsseldorfer Schauspielhaus, 1994

RSC, 1984

RSC, 1995

National Theatre, 2000

ACT 4   SCENE 1

In this scene ...

- Juliet arrives at the Friar's cell. After a brief conversation with Paris, she asks the Friar for help.
- Seeing how desperate Juliet is, the Friar suggests a plan. Juliet is to take a potion which will make it appear as though she is dead. She will be laid in the Capulet tomb. The Friar will write to Romeo, who can then come and collect her secretly. She eagerly agrees.

Juliet arrives at the Friar's cell just as Paris is discussing arrangements for the wedding.

Think about

- What have the Friar and Paris been talking about before the scene begins? What might have been in the Friar's mind when Paris arrived?

- What do Juliet and the Friar mean by 'What must be shall be. / That's a certain text.' (line 21)? How do their words tie in with the theme of fate running through the play?

2   **father**: i.e. father-in-law to be

3   **nothing ... haste**: very keen not to slow him down

5   **Uneven ... course**: This is an irregular way of going about things

8   **Venus ... tears**: i.e. people in mourning do not want to think about love

9   **counts**: considers

10 **do give ... sway**: gives way to her sorrow so much

12 **inundation**: flood

13 **minded**: thought about

14 **put ... society**: driven away by company

16 **would**: wish

18 **Happily**: Fortunately

21 **certain text**: true saying

Friar Lawrence's cell.

Enter FRIAR LAWRENCE, *with Count* PARIS.

FR. LAWRENCE	On Thursday, sir? The time is very short.
PARIS	My father Capulet will have it so,
	And I am nothing slow to slack his haste.
FR. LAWRENCE	You say you do not know the lady's mind?
	Uneven is the course: I like it not.

5

PARIS	Immoderately she weeps for Tybalt's death,
	And therefore have I little talked of love,
	For Venus smiles not in a house of tears.
	Now, sir, her father counts it dangerous
	That she do give her sorrow so much sway,

10

	And in his wisdom hastes our marriage,
	To stop the inundation of her tears –
	Which, too much minded by herself alone,
	May be put from her by society.
	Now do you know the reason of this haste.

15

FR. LAWRENCE	*(Aside)* I would I knew not why it should be slowed. –
	Look, sir, here comes the lady toward my cell.

Enter JULIET.

PARIS	Happily met, my lady and my wife!
JULIET	That may be, sir, when I may be a wife.
PARIS	That 'may be' must be, love, on Thursday next.

20

JULIET	What must be shall be.
FR. LAWRENCE	That's a certain text.
PARIS	Come you to make confession to this father?
JULIET	To answer that, I should confess to you.
PARIS	Do not deny to him that you love me.
JULIET	I will confess to you that I love him.

25

Juliet responds coldly to Paris's words of love. When Paris leaves, she begs the Friar's help, threatening to kill herself immediately if all else fails.

27 **price**: value

29 **abused**: spoiled

31 **spite**: meanness in harming it

33 **slander**: unfair criticism
34 **to my face**: 1 about my face; 2 openly

39 **My leisure serves me**: I am free
    pensive: 1 thoughtful; 2 sad
40 **entreat**: ask for
41 **shield**: forbid

Think about

• What is your opinion of Paris's behaviour with Juliet? Think about whether he seems over-possessive, for example, or if he is simply behaving as a fiancé should.

• How do you think Paris might feel when he thinks back to this meeting with the Friar and Juliet? How might he interpret Juliet's behaviour?

46 **thy grief**: the cause of your grief
47 **It strains ... wits**: I have racked my brains without success
48 **prorogue**: postpone

53 **resolution**: determination
54 **presently**: at once

56 **ere**: before
    sealed: joined

PARIS	So will ye, I am sure, that you love me.
JULIET	If I do so, it will be of more price,
	Being spoke behind your back, than to your face.
PARIS	Poor soul, thy face is much abused with tears.
JULIET	The tears have got small victory by that,
	For it was bad enough before their spite.
PARIS	Thou wrong'st it more than tears with that report.
JULIET	That is no slander, sir, which is a truth,
	And what I spake, I spake it to my face.
PARIS	Thy face is mine, and thou hast slandered it.
JULIET	It may be so, for it is not mine own. –
	Are you at leisure, holy Father, now,
	Or shall I come to you at evening mass?
FR. LAWRENCE	My leisure serves me, pensive daughter, now.
	My lord, we must entreat the time alone.
PARIS	God shield I should disturb devotion.
	Juliet, on Thursday early will I rouse ye –
	Till then, adieu, and keep this holy kiss.

He kisses her.

Exit.

JULIET	O, shut the door, and when thou hast done so,
	Come weep with me – past hope, past cure, past help!
FR. LAWRENCE	O Juliet, I already know thy grief –
	It strains me past the compass of my wits.
	I hear thou must – and nothing may prorogue it –
	On Thursday next be married to this County.
JULIET	Tell me not, Friar, that thou hearest of this,
	Unless thou tell me how I may prevent it.
	If in thy wisdom thou canst give no help,
	Do thou but call my resolution wise,
	And with this knife I'll help it presently.
	God joined my heart and Romeo's, thou our hands.
	And ere this hand, by thee to Romeo's sealed,

30

35

40

45

50

55

Juliet declares that she will go along with any plan of the Friar's, however desperate. He gives her a potion.

Think about

- How could the actor playing Juliet perform lines 44 to 88? In particular, what could she do at line 62?

- What might the Friar be thinking as Juliet speaks? Think about how he arrives at the plan he tells Juliet about from line 89, for example.

57 **label ... deed**: seal to another marriage contract

59 **this**: i.e. the knife

60 **time**: life

61 **present counsel**: immediate advice

62 **'Twixt ... me**: between me and the desperate situation I am in

63 **arbitrating**: making a final decision about

64 **commission**: authority
art: skill

65 **issue ... honour**: honourable conclusion

68 **Hold**: Wait

69 **craves ... execution**: requires you to do something as desperate

70 **that ... prevent**: i.e. killing yourself or committing bigamy

74 **chide away**: i.e. drive off

75 **cop'st with**: i.e. are prepared to face
scape from it: escape from the disgrace of marrying Paris

79 **thievish ways**: places where you find thieves

81 **charnel house**: building in which old skulls and bones were stored when new graves were being dug in the churchyard

83 **reeky shanks**: stinking shin-bones
chapless: with lower jaws missing

85 **shroud**: sheet in which the corpse was wrapped

88 **unstained**: pure / chaste

91 **look ... lie**: make sure you sleep

93 **vial**: small bottle / flask

94 **distilling**: refined into a spirit

95 **presently**: immediately

	Shall be the label to another deed,
	Or my true heart with treacherous revolt
	Turn to another, this shall slay them both!
	Therefore, out of thy long-experienced time,
	Give me some present counsel – or, behold,
	'Twixt my extremes and me, this bloody knife
	Shall play the umpire, arbitrating that
	Which the commission of thy years and art
	Could to no issue of true honour bring.
	Be not so long to speak. I long to die –
	If what thou speak'st speak not of remedy.

FR. LAWRENCE Hold, daughter. – I do spy a kind of hope,
Which craves as desperate an execution
As that is desperate which we would prevent.   70
If, rather than to marry County Paris,
Thou hast the strength of will to slay thyself,
Then is it likely thou wilt undertake
A thing *like* death to chide away this shame –
That cop'st with death himself to scape from it.   75
And, if thou dar'st, I'll give thee remedy.

JULIET O, bid me leap, rather than marry Paris,
From off the battlements of any tower –
Or walk in thievish ways, or bid me lurk
Where serpents are! Chain me with roaring bears,   80
Or hide me nightly in a charnel house,
O'ercovered quite with dead men's rattling bones,
With reeky shanks and yellow chapless skulls!
Or bid me go into a new-made grave,
And hide me with a dead man in his shroud! –   85
Things that, to hear them told, have made me tremble –
And I will do it, without fear or doubt,
To live an unstained wife to my sweet love.

FR. LAWRENCE Hold, then. Go home, be merry, give consent
To marry Paris. Wednesday is tomorrow.   90
Tomorrow night look that thou lie alone.
Let not the Nurse lie with thee in thy chamber.
Take thou this vial, being then in bed,
And this distilling liquor drink thou off –
When presently through all thy veins shall run   95

60
65

197

The potion will cause Juliet to seem dead. She will be placed in the Capulet tomb and, when she wakes, can go with Romeo to Mantua. Juliet readily agrees and the Friar promises to send letters to tell Romeo what is going on.

96 **humour**: fluid
97 **native progress**: natural rate
surcease: stop
98 **testify**: give evidence that
100 **wanny**: pale
windows: shutters (i.e. lids)
102 **supple government**: control of movement
104 **borrowed likeness**: imitation

108 **there … dead**: they will find you (apparently) dead
109 **manner**: custom
110 **uncovered**: with your face uncovered
bier: funeral carriage
113 **against**: in preparation for the time when
114 **drift**: intentions
116 **watch thy waking**: watch over you until you wake up
117 **bear thee hence**: carry you off
119 **inconstant toy**: whim making you change your mind
120 **Abate**: lessen
valour: courage
122 **prosperous**: fortunate

125 **afford**: provide

Think about

• What are the strengths and weaknesses of the Friar's plan? How far is he protecting himself, do you think?

• What does Juliet's reaction to the plan at line 121 reveal about her?

A cold and drowsy humour: for no pulse
Shall keep his native progress, but surcease.
No warmth, no breath, shall testify thou livest.
The roses in thy lips and cheeks shall fade
To wanny ashes, thy eyes' windows fall   100
Like death when he shuts up the day of life.
Each part, deprived of supple government,
Shall, stiff and stark and cold, appear like death,
And in this borrowed likeness of shrunk death
Thou shalt continue two and forty hours –   105
And then awake as from a pleasant sleep.
Now, when the bridegroom in the morning comes
To rouse thee from thy bed, there art thou, dead.
Then, as the manner of our country is,
In thy best robes, uncovered on the bier,   110
Thou shalt be borne to that same ancient vault
Where all the kindred of the Capulets lie.
In the meantime, against thou shalt awake,
Shall Romeo by my letters know our drift,
And hither shall he come. And he and I   115
Will watch thy waking, and that very night
Shall Romeo bear thee hence to Mantua.
And this shall free thee from this present shame,
If no inconstant toy nor womanish fear
Abate thy valour in the acting it.   120

JULIET   Give me, give me! O, tell not me of fear!

FR. LAWRENCE Hold. Get you gone. Be strong and prosperous
In this resolve. I'll send a friar with speed
To Mantua, with my letters to thy lord.

JULIET   Love give me strength! – and strength shall help afford! 125
Farewell, dear Father!

Exeunt.

In this scene ...

- Juliet returns home and tells her father that she has seen the Friar and is now sorry for her disobedience.
- Capulet excitedly gives instructions that the wedding will now take place the following day and goes to inform Paris.

Juliet returns home to find her father making preparations for the wedding. She says that, after speaking to the Friar, she wishes to ask forgiveness for her earlier disobedience.

2   **cunning**: skilful

3   **none ill:** no bad ones
try: test

6–7   **lick ... fingers**: i.e. it shows that they are confident in their own cooking

10   **much unfurnished**: extremely unprepared

12   **Ay, forsooth**: She certainly has

14   **A peevish ... is**: She is a moody, stubborn little good-for-nothing

15   **shrift**: confession

16   **gadding**: running around enjoying yourself

Think about

- What does Capulet's dialogue with the servants (lines 1 to 9) add to the beginning of this scene? In productions it is often cut. What would be gained and lost by cutting it?

19   **behests**: commands
enjoined: instructed

200

The Capulet house.

Enter CAPULET, LADY CAPULET, *the* NURSE, *and three* SERVANTS.

CAPULET	(*Giving a paper to a servant*) So many guests invite as here are writ.

Exit SERVANT.

	(*To another* SERVANT) Sirrah, go hire me twenty cunning cooks.
SERVANT	You shall have none ill, sir, for I'll try if they can lick their fingers.
CAPULET	How canst thou try them so?

5

SERVANT	Marry, sir, 'tis an ill cook that cannot lick his own fingers! Therefore he that cannot lick his own fingers goes not with me.
CAPULET	Go, be gone.

Exit SERVANT.

	We shall be much unfurnished for this time.

10

What, is my daughter gone to Friar Lawrence?

NURSE	Ay, forsooth.
CAPULET	Well, he may chance to do some good on her.

A peevish, self-willed harlotry it is!

Enter JULIET.

NURSE	See where she comes from shrift with merry look.

15

CAPULET	How now, my headstrong? Where have you been gadding?
JULIET	(*Kneeling to her father*) Where I have learnt me to repent the sin

Of disobedient opposition
To you and your behests, and am enjoined

Capulet is so delighted at Juliet's change of heart that he gives orders for the wedding to take place the following day. He joyfully promises to oversee the wedding preparations himself and bustles off to inform Paris.

20 **fall prostrate**: i.e. kneel down

22 **am ever … you**: will always do as you say

24 **this knot**: i.e. the 'marriage-knot'

26 **becomèd**: appropriate
27 **stepping … modesty**: doing anything improper

32 **is … to him**: owes him a great debt
33 **closet**: private room
34 **sort**: select
    needful: necessary
35 **to furnish me**: for me to wear

38 **be … provision**: not have enough food ready

39 **Tush**: Nonsense
    stir about: stay up and get things done
40 **warrant**: assure
41 **deck up**: dress
42 **Let me alone**: Leave everything to me

44 **forth**: out of the house

46 **Against**: for
47 **reclaimed**: i.e. obedient once again

Think about

• What advice would you give to the actor playing Capulet on how he should (a) behave with the servants (lines 1 to 9); (b) talk about Juliet before she enters (lines 11 to 14); (c) address Juliet (line 16); and (d) react to her (lines 23 to 24, 28 to 32, and 37)?

	By holy Lawrence to fall prostrate here	**20**
	To beg your pardon. Pardon, I beseech you!	
	Henceforward I am ever ruled by you.	

CAPULET   Send for the County! Go, tell him of this.
I'll have this knot knit up tomorrow morning!

JULIET   I met the youthful lord at Lawrence' cell,   **25**
And gave him what becomèd love I might,
Not stepping o'er the bounds of modesty.

CAPULET   Why, I am glad on't! This is well. Stand up.
This is as 't should be. Let me see the County! –
Ay, marry, go, I say, and fetch him hither.   **30**
Now, afore God, this reverend holy Friar –
All our whole city is much bound to him!

JULIET   Nurse, will you go with me into my closet
To help me sort such needful ornaments
As you think fit to furnish me tomorrow?   **35**

LADY CAPULET   No, not till Thursday. There is time enough.

CAPULET   Go, Nurse, go with her. We'll to church tomorrow.

Exit JULIET, *with the* NURSE.

LADY CAPULET   We shall be short in our provision.
'Tis now near night.

CAPULET   Tush, I will stir about,
And all things shall be well, I warrant thee, wife.   **40**
Go thou to Juliet. Help to deck up her.
I'll not to bed tonight. Let me alone –
I'll play the housewife for this once! (*Calling for the
   servants*) What ho! –
They are all forth. – Well, I will walk myself
To County Paris, to prepare up him   **45**
Against tomorrow. My heart is wondrous light
Since this same wayward girl is so reclaimed!

Exeunt.

In this scene ...

- Juliet prepares for bed and says goodnight to her mother and the Nurse.
- Juliet overcomes her fears and drinks the potion.

Juliet says goodnight to her mother and the Nurse. Left alone, she anxiously thinks about what might happen if the potion does not work. It occurs to her that the Friar might be trying to poison her, to avoid having to marry her a second time, illegally.

Think about

- The Nurse thinks that Juliet is going to marry Paris even though she is already married to Romeo, committing both a serious crime and a sin. Shakespeare gives her no lines here, but what might she be thinking?

- Lady Capulet says very little, but how should she behave towards Juliet, and how should her daughter react to her? Think about their earlier behaviour.

1 **attires**: clothes

3 **orisons**: prayers
4 **move**: persuade
   state: situation
5 **cross**: wrong

7 **culled such necessaries**: selected what we need
8 **behoveful**: suitable and needed
   state: wedding ceremony

12 **sudden**: unexpectedly quick

15 **faint cold**: causing faintness and chill
    thrills: shivers

19 **dismal**: dreadful
20 **vial**: small bottle / flask (containing the potion)

25 **Subtly hath ministered**: has cunningly prescribed for me
26 **Lest ... dishonoured**: for fear of his being disgraced by this wedding

Juliet's bedroom.

Enter JULIET *and the* NURSE.

JULIET	Ay, those attires are best. But, gentle Nurse,
	I pray thee leave me to myself tonight,
	For I have need of many orisons
	To move the heavens to smile upon my state,
	Which well thou knowest is cross and full of sin.

5

Enter LADY CAPULET.

LADY CAPULET	What, are you busy, ho? Need you my help?
JULIET	No, madam – we have culled such necessaries
	As are behoveful for our state tomorrow.
	So please you, let me now be left alone,
	And let the Nurse this night sit up with you –
	For I am sure you have your hands full all
	In this so sudden business.

10

LADY CAPULET	Good night.
	Get thee to bed and rest, for thou hast need.

Exit, with the NURSE.

JULIET	Farewell. – God knows when we shall meet again.
	I have a faint cold fear thrills through my veins,
	That almost freezes up the heat of life.
	I'll call them back again to comfort me.
	(*She calls*) Nurse! – What should she do here?
	My dismal scene I needs must act alone.
	Come, vial.
	What if this mixture do not work at all?
	Shall I be married then tomorrow morning?
	No, no. – (*Taking out her knife*) This shall forbid it.
	(*Placing the knife inside the curtain by her bed*)
	Lie thou there.
	What if it be a poison which the Friar
	Subtly hath ministered to have me dead,
	Lest in this marriage he should be dishonoured

15

20

25

Juliet is terrified at the thought of suffocating in the tomb, or going mad with fear when she wakes to find herself surrounded by bones. Imagining Tybalt's ghost looking for Romeo, she drinks the potion.

29 **still been tried**: always proved to be

32 **redeem**: rescue
33 **stifled**: suffocated
34 **healthsome**: fresh / wholesome
35 **strangled ere**: choked before

37 **conceit**: thoughts / idea

39 **receptacle**: collecting place

42 **green in earth**: newly buried
43 **shroud**: burial sheet
44 **resort**: gather

47 **mandrakes**: roots shaped like a man (It was believed that, if someone pulled one out of the ground, it would scream and the person would go mad.)
49 **distraught**: driven mad
50 **Environed with**: surrounded by
53 **rage**: madness

56 **spit**: pierce / skewer
57 **Stay**: Stop

Think about

• Juliet's fears seem like nightmares. Which of her descriptions do you find most effective here?

• How is language used to (a) describe the terrifying scenes she is imagining; and (b) convey her fear? Look, for example, at verb tenses, the repetition of 'I', choice of vocabulary, and her description of imagined situations.

Because he married me before to Romeo?
I fear it is. And yet methinks it should not,
For he hath still been tried a holy man.
How if, when I am laid into the tomb,   30
I wake before the time that Romeo
Come to redeem me? There's a fearful point!
Shall I not then be stifled in the vault,
To whose foul mouth no healthsome air breathes in,
And there die strangled ere my Romeo comes?   35
Or, if I live, is it not very like
The horrible conceit of death and night,
Together with the terror of the place –
As in a vault, an ancient receptacle,
Where, for this many hundred years, the bones   40
Of all my buried ancestors are packed –
Where bloody Tybalt, yet but green in earth,
Lies festering in his shroud – where, as they say,
At some hours in the night spirits resort –
Alack, alack! – Is it not like that I,   45
So early waking – what with loathsome smells,
And shrieks like mandrakes torn out of the earth,
That living mortals, hearing them run mad –
O! – If I wake, shall I not be distraught,
Environed with all these hideous fears,   50
And madly play with my forefathers' joints,
And pluck the mangled Tybalt from his shroud! –
And in this rage, with some great kinsman's bone,
As with a club, dash out my desperate brains?
O look! – Methinks I see my cousin's ghost,   55
Seeking out Romeo that did spit his body
Upon a rapier's point. Stay, Tybalt! Stay! –
Romeo! Romeo, Romeo! Here's drink! – I drink to thee!

She drinks the drug and falls onto her bed.

In this scene ...

- Early next morning the household is busy preparing for the wedding when music is heard outside: Paris has arrived to take Juliet to church.

At three o'clock in the morning, Capulet is fussily supervising last-minute preparations for the wedding.

2 **pastry**: pastry-room in the kitchen

3 **stir**: get a move on
4 **curfew bell**: bell rung when the watch patrol went on or off duty
5 **baked meats**: pies
   Angelica: probably the Nurse's name
6 **cot-quean**: man who interferes with household matters (a woman's job in those days)
8 **watching**: staying awake
9 **not a whit**: not at all

11 **mouse-hunt**: i.e. woman-chaser
12 **watch you**: keep an eye on you

13 **jealous-hood**: jealous woman

Think about

- What does the exchange between Capulet and the Nurse (lines 5 to 10) suggest about their relationship?

- In what tone should Lady Capulet say lines 11 and 12? Should she be joking, bitter, threatening, or something else?

The great hall of the Capulet house.

Enter Lady Capulet *with the* Nurse *(carrying a basket of herbs).*

LADY CAPULET   Hold, take these keys and fetch more spices, Nurse.

NURSE   They call for dates and quinces in the pastry.

Enter Capulet.

CAPULET   Come, stir, stir, stir! The second cock hath crowed,
The curfew bell hath rung, 'tis three o'clock.
Look to the baked meats, good Angelica! –   5
Spare not for cost.

NURSE   Go, you cot-quean, go!
Get you to bed. Faith, you'll be sick to-morrow
For this night's watching.

CAPULET   No, not a whit. What! I have watched ere now
All night for lesser cause and ne'er been sick.   10

LADY CAPULET   Ay, you have been a mouse-hunt in your time,
But I will watch you from such watching now.

Exit, with the NURSE.

CAPULET   A jealous-hood, a jealous-hood!

Enter three SERVANTS, *carrying cooking-spits, firewood, and baskets.*

Now, fellow, what is there?

SERVANT   Things for the cook, sir, but I know not what.

CAPULET   Make haste, make haste, sirrah! Fetch drier logs.   15
Call Peter – he will show thee where they are.

Exit SERVANT. *Another follows.*

SERVANT   I have a head, sir, that will find out logs –
And never trouble Peter for the matter.

Hearing Paris approach with the musicians, Capulet tells the Nurse to hurry off and wake Juliet up.

19 **Mass**: By the mass (a common oath)
    whoreson: rogue
20 **loggerhead**: blockhead
21 **straight**: straight away

24 **trim her up**: get her ready

Think about

- Very little happens in this scene, so what are its purposes? Compare it with the scenes which come before and after it, for example.

CAPULET   Mass, and well said! – a merry whoreson, ha!
           Thou shalt be loggerhead! (*Exit* SERVANT) – Good faith,
             'tis day!   **20**
           The County will be here with music straight,
           For so he said he would. (*Faint sounds of music are
             heard*) – I hear him near.
           Nurse! Wife! What ho! What, Nurse, I say!

Enter the NURSE.

           Go waken Juliet! – go, and trim her up.
           I'll go and chat with Paris. Hie, make haste,   **25**
           Make haste! The bridegroom he is come already.
           Make haste, I say!

                                                        Exit.

                    The NURSE *goes directly to Juliet's bedroom.*

In this scene ...

- When the Nurse goes to wake Juliet, she finds her apparently dead.
- Paris and the Friar enter to find the Capulets grief-stricken over Juliet's death.
- As the family go off to prepare for a funeral, Peter jokes with the musicians.

The Nurse comes to wake Juliet, but the potion has worked and Juliet appears to be dead.

1 **Fast**: Fast asleep

4 **pennyworths**: small quantities (i.e. what little sleep you can get)
6 **set up his rest**: made up his mind

10 **take you**: 1 find you; 2 have sex with you
11 **fright you up**: frighten you into getting up
12 **down again**: lying down on your bed again
13 **I must needs**: I'll have to
15 **well-a-day**: an expression of grief
16 **aqua-vitae**: strong spirits (brandy)

20 **look up**: open your eyes

Think about

- On stage there are many ways in which the Nurse can come to realise that Juliet is 'dead'. Do you think she should realise gradually or suddenly? When does she know for certain?

ACT 4   SCENE 5

Juliet's bedroom.

NURSE   (*Going in and calling*) Mistress! What, mistress! – Fast,
                   I warrant her, she.
                   Why, lamb! Why, lady! Fie, you slug-a-bed!
                   Why, love, I say! Madam! Sweetheart! Why, bride!
                   What, not a word? You take your pennyworths now.
                   Sleep for a week – for the next night, I warrant,   5
                   The County Paris hath set up his rest
                   That you shall rest but little. – God forgive me!
                   Marry, and amen! How sound is she asleep!
                   I needs must wake her. Madam, madam, madam!
                   Ay – let the County take you in your bed –   10
                   He'll fright you up, i' faith. Will it not be?

She pulls aside the bed-curtain.

                   What, dressed, and in your clothes, and down again?
                   I must needs wake you. Lady, lady, lady!
                   Alas, alas! Help, help! My lady's dead!
                   O well-a-day that ever I was born!   15
                   Some aqua-vitae, ho! My lord! My lady!

Enter LADY CAPULET.

LADY CAPULET What noise is here?

NURSE   O lamentable day!

LADY CAPULET What is the matter?

NURSE   Look, look! O heavy day!

LADY CAPULET O me, O me! My child, my only life!
                   Revive, look up, or I will die with thee!   20
                   Help, help! Call help!

Enter CAPULET.

CAPULET   For shame, bring Juliet forth. Her lord is come.

NURSE   She's dead, deceased! She's dead, alack the day!

LADY CAPULET Alack the day, she's dead, she's dead, she's dead!

Paris arrives with the Friar, to find Juliet's parents grieving at their daughter's death.

26 is settled: has stopped flowing

28 untimely: out of season (i.e. too early)

36 lain with: had sex with
37 deflowerèd by him: lost her virginity to him (i.e. death)

40 living: property
41 thought long: i.e. been impatient

Think about

• What might each of the following characters be thinking at the moment the Friar enters with Paris (line 32): Capulet, Lady Capulet, the Nurse, the Friar, and Paris?

• What picture of Death does Capulet seem to have formed? Look at lines 28 to 29, and 31 to 40.

45 lasting ... pilgrimage: the unending toil of his journey
46 But one: I had only one
47 solace: find comfort
48 catched: snatched

CAPULET	Ha, let me see her! Out, alas! She's cold! –	25
	Her blood is settled, and her joints are stiff.	
	Life and these lips have long been separated.	
	Death lies on her like an untimely frost	
	Upon the sweetest flower of all the field.	

NURSE   O lamentable day!

LADY CAPULET   O woeful time!   30

CAPULET   Death, that hath ta'en her hence to make me wail,
          Ties up my tongue and will not let me speak.

Enter FRIAR LAWRENCE *and Count* PARIS, *followed by* MUSICIANS,
for the wedding.

FR. LAWRENCE   Come, is the bride ready to go to church?

CAPULET   Ready to go, but never to return.
          O son, the night before thy wedding day   35
          Hath Death lain with thy wife. There she lies,
          Flower as she was, deflowerèd by him.
          Death is my son-in-law, Death is my heir.
          My daughter he hath wedded. I will die
          And leave him all. Life, living – all is Death's!   40

PARIS   Have I thought long to see this morning's face,
          And doth it give me such a sight as this?

LADY CAPULET   Accursed, unhappy, wretched, hateful day!
          Most miserable hour that e'er time saw
          In lasting labour of his pilgrimage.   45
          But one, poor one, one poor and loving child –
          But one thing to rejoice and solace in,
          And cruel Death hath catched it from my sight!

NURSE   O woe! O woeful, woeful, woeful day!
          Most lamentable day, most woeful day   50
          That ever, ever I did yet behold!
          O day, O day, O day, O hateful day!
          Never was seen so black a day as this.
          O woeful day, O woeful day!

The Friar tries to stop people grieving, offering them the comfort that Juliet is now in heaven. Capulet prepares for a funeral rather than the expected wedding.

Think about

- What do the Friar's words of consolation (lines 65 to 83) reveal about attitudes to death in Shakespeare's time?

- The commonest words in Capulet's two speeches (lines 59 to 64, and 84 to 90) are 'my' and 'our'. What might that suggest about his reaction to Juliet's supposed death?

55 **Beguiled**: Cheated

59 **martyred**: punished by death
60 **Uncomfortable**: Pitiless
61 **murder our solemnity**: ruin our wedding feast with death

65 **Confusion's cure**: The cure for your great loss
66 **confusions**: wild cries of grief
67 **part**: a share
70 **his part**: i.e. her soul
71 **promotion**: moving up in the world (by marrying Paris)
72 **heaven**: i.e. greatest happiness
be advanced: move higher up in society
75 **this love**: i.e. the love that mourns her death
76 **well**: happy (often used of those who are dead)
77–8 **She's not ... young** : i.e. a woman who dies young is best 'married' to heaven
79 **rosemary**: the herb of remembrance, used at weddings and funerals
80 **corse**: corpse
81 **array**: clothes
82 **fond ... lament**: foolish (and too affectionate) natural feelings cause us to grieve
83 **nature's ... merriment**: i.e. it is natural to cry but not sensible, as she is in heaven
84 **ordainèd festival**: i.e. the wedding plans
85 **office**: usual function
87 **cheer**: banquet
88 **sullen dirges**: mournful funeral hymns
90 **contrary**: opposite

PARIS	Beguiled, divorcèd, wrongèd, spited, slain!	55
	Most detestable Death, by thee beguiled –	
	By cruel, cruel thee quite overthrown!	
	O love! O life! – Not life, but love in death!	

PARIS   Beguiled, divorcèd, wrongèd, spited, slain!   55
Most detestable Death, by thee beguiled –
By cruel, cruel thee quite overthrown!
O love! O life! – Not life, but love in death!

CAPULET   Despised, distressèd, hated, martyred, killed!
Uncomfortable time, why cam'st thou now   60
To murder, murder our solemnity?
O child, O child! My soul, and not my child!
Dead art thou. Alack, my child is dead,
And with my child my joys are burièd.

FR. LAWRENCE   Peace, ho, for shame! Confusion's cure lives not   65
In these confusions. Heaven and yourself
Had part in this fair maid: now heaven hath all,
And all the better is it for the maid.
Your part in her you could not keep from death,
But heaven keeps his part in eternal life.   70
The most you sought was her promotion,
For 'twas your heaven she should be advanced.
And weep ye now, seeing she is advanced
Above the clouds, as high as heaven itself?
O, in this love you love your child so ill   75
That you run mad, seeing that she is well.
She's not well married that lives married long,
But she's best married that dies married young.
Dry up your tears, and stick your rosemary
On this fair corse, and, as the custom is,   80
In all her best array bear her to church.
For though fond nature bids us all lament,
Yet nature's tears are reason's merriment.

CAPULET   All things that we ordainèd festival
Turn from their office to black funeral: 85
Our instruments to melancholy bells,
Our wedding cheer to a sad burial feast,
Our solemn hymns to sullen dirges change,
Our bridal flowers serve for a buried corse,
And all things change them to the contrary.   90

As the family leave, Peter asks the musicians to play something to console him. He then engages in some wordplay with them.

94 **lour**: look angrily
ill: sin
95 **Move**: anger
crossing: defying / going against

96 **may ... gone**: might as well pack up

98 **case**: state of affairs

99 **case may be amended**: 1 things could be better; 2 my instrument case needs repairing

100 **Heart's ease**: a popular song of the time
101 **and**: if

104 **dump**: sad tune

105 **Not ... we**: We're not playing a sad tune
108 **give ... soundly**: pay you out in full
110 **gleek**: gibe / jeer
110–11 **give ... minstrel**: call you worthless wandering musicians (an insult)
112 **serving-creature**: more insulting than 'serving-man'
114 **pate**: head
carry no crotchets: not put up with any of your games (crotchets are musical notes)
re ... fa: musical notes
114–15 **Do you note me**: Are you paying attention

Think about

• In lines 100 to 104 Peter seems to be sad at Juliet's death, but he soon switches to wordplay with the musicians. How should the actor play this scene, do you think? Should he be sad, but attempting to cover it, for example, or not really affected at all?

FR. LAWRENCE   Sir, go you in. And, madam, go with him;
                And go, Sir Paris. Everyone prepare
                To follow this fair corse unto her grave.
                The heavens do lour upon you for some ill:
                Move them no more by crossing their high will.   95

They sadly scatter rosemary around JULIET*'s body, and close
the bed-curtain.*

                    All exit, except the NURSE, *and the* MUSICIANS,
                                        who remain by the door.

MUSICIAN 1   Faith, we may put up our pipes and be gone.

NURSE   Honest good fellows – ah, put up, put up –
              For well you know this is a pitiful case.

MUSICIAN 1   Ay, by my troth, the case may be amended.

                                        Exit the NURSE.

Enter PETER.

PETER   Musicians, O musicians, 'Heart's ease', 'Heart's ease'! 100
              O, and you will have me live, play 'Heart's ease'!

MUSICIAN 1   Why 'Heart's ease'?

PETER   O musicians, because my heart itself plays 'My heart is
              full'. O, play me some merry dump to comfort me.

MUSICIAN 1   Not a dump, we. 'Tis no time to play now.   105

PETER   You will not then?

MUSICIAN 1   No.

PETER   I will then give it you soundly.

MUSICIAN 1   What will you give us?

PETER   No money, on my faith, but the gleek. I will give you the 110
              minstrel.

MUSICIAN 1   Then will I give *you* the serving-creature.

PETER   Then will I lay the serving-creature's dagger on your
              pate. I will carry no crotchets. I'll re you, I'll fa you! Do
              you note me?   115

Peter continues to joke with the musicians. They decide to wait for the mourners to return from the funeral and then join them for dinner.

116 note us: 1 pay attention to us; 2 set us to music

117 put up: put away
put out: display

118 dry-beat you: beat you up without drawing blood

119 iron wit: i.e. 'killing', merciless wit

121–3 When ... sound: the last few lines of a poem in praise of music

125 Catling: lute-string (made of cat-gut)

127 Pretty: Nice answer
Rebeck: three-stringed fiddle

128 sound for silver: play for money

129 Soundpost: support inside a stringed instrument

131 cry you mercy: beg your pardon
You ... singer: i.e. you aren't much of a speaker

133 for sounding: 1 as payment for playing; 2 to jingle in their purses

135 lend redress: put things right

136 pestilent knave: wretched nuisance

137 Jack: rogue
tarry: linger

138 stay: wait for

Think about

- In most productions this section with the musicians (lines 96 to 138) is cut. What purpose does it serve? What is gained and lost by cutting it?

MUSICIAN 1	And you re us and fa us, you note us.
MUSICIAN 2	Pray you, put up your dagger, and put out your wit.
PETER	Then have at you with my wit! I will dry-beat you with an iron wit, and put up my iron dagger. Answer me like men:

120

> 'When griping grief the heart doth wound,
> And doleful dumps the mind oppress,
> Then music with her silver sound –'

Why 'silver sound'? Why 'music with her silver sound'?
What say you, Simon Catling?

125

MUSICIAN 1	Marry, sir, because silver hath a sweet sound.
PETER	Pretty! What say you, Hugh Rebeck?
MUSICIAN 2	I say 'silver sound' because musicians sound for silver.
PETER	Pretty too! What say you, James Soundpost?
MUSICIAN 3	Faith, I know not what to say.

130

PETER	O, I cry you mercy! You are the singer. I will say for you. It is 'music with her *silver* sound' because musicians have no gold for sounding!

> '– Then music with her silver sound
> With speedy help doth lend redress.'

135

Exit PETER.

MUSICIAN 1	What a pestilent knave is this same!
MUSICIAN 2	Hang him, Jack! Come, we'll in here, tarry for the mourners, and stay dinner.

Exeunt.

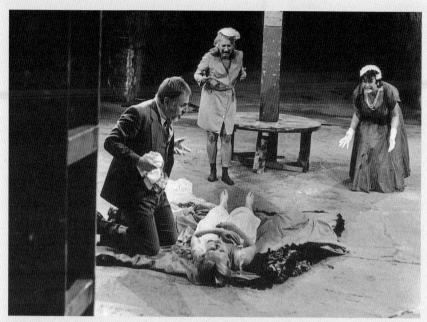

Northern Broadsides, 1996

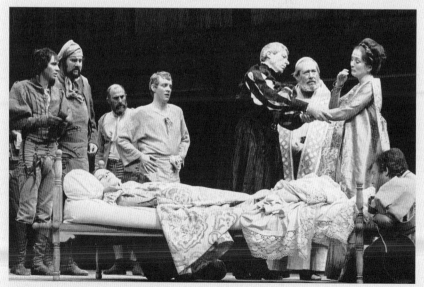

RSC, 1976

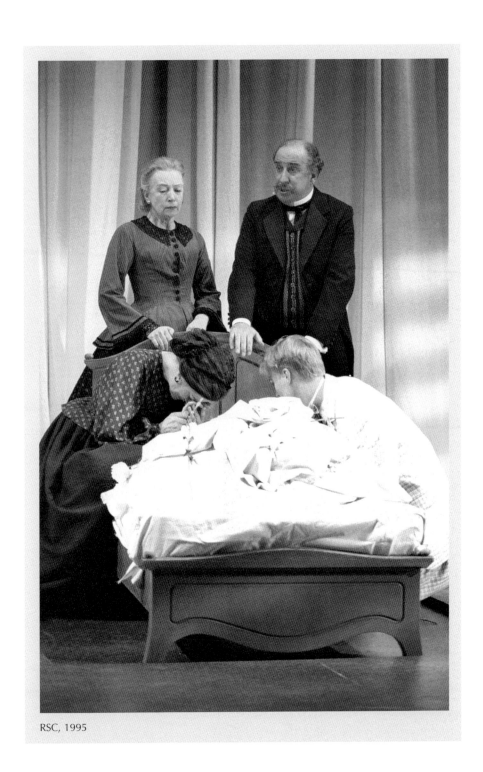

RSC, 1995

ACT 5   SCENE 1

In this scene ...

- Balthasar brings news to Romeo in Mantua that Juliet is dead.
- In desperation, Romeo vows to be with Juliet that night.
- He buys poison from an Apothecary and leaves for Verona.

In Mantua, Romeo thinks about a dream which has made him feel happier. But he is devastated when Balthasar brings news that Juliet is dead, her body lying in the Capulet tomb.

Think about

- What do you think Romeo means by 'Then I defy you, stars!' (line 24)? What is he thinking about? Why does he express himself in this way?

- What attitude does Romeo seem to have towards fate? Look back at Act 3 Scene 1, line 132 (O, I am fortune's fool!), for example.

1 **flattering**: i.e. because dreams often tell us what we want to believe
2 **presage**: foretell
3 **My bosom's ... throne**: i.e. my heart is full of love
4 **unaccustomed spirit**: unusual feeling
7 **leave**: permission

10 **itself possessed**: enjoyed in reality
11 **love's shadows**: dreams of love

17 **well**: happy (often used of those who are dead)
18 **Capel's monument**: the Capulet tomb
19 **immortal part**: soul
20 **kindred**: family
21 **presently took post**: rode here straight away
23 **for my office**: as my duty
24 **Is it e'en so**: Is that the way things are

26 **post-horses**: the fastest means of transport
28-9 **import ... misadventure**: suggest some future disaster

224

A street in Mantua.

Enter ROMEO.

ROMEO	If I may trust the flattering truth of sleep,
	My dreams presage some joyful news at hand.
	My bosom's lord sits lightly in his throne,
	And all this day an unaccustomed spirit
	Lifts me above the ground with cheerful thoughts.

5

I dreamt my lady came and found me dead –
Strange dream, that gives a dead man leave to think! –
And breathed such life with kisses in my lips
That I revived and was an emperor.
Ah me! How sweet is love itself possessed,

10

When but love's shadows are so rich in joy!

Enter BALTHASAR *(Romeo's servant), in riding-boots.*

News from Verona! How now, Balthasar?
Dost thou not bring me letters from the Friar?
How doth my lady? Is my father well?
How fares my Juliet? That I ask again,

15

For nothing can be ill if she be well.

BALTHASAR Then she is well, and nothing can be ill.
Her body sleeps in Capel's monument,
And her immortal part with angels lives.
I saw her laid low in her kindred's vault,

20

And presently took post to tell it you.
O pardon me for bringing these ill news,
Since you did leave it for my office, sir.

ROMEO Is it e'en so? Then I defy you, stars!
Thou know'st my lodging. Get me ink and paper –

25

And hire post-horses. I will hence tonight.

BALTHASAR I do beseech you, sir, have patience.
Your looks are pale and wild, and do import
Some misadventure.

Balthasar confirms that he has not brought a letter from the Friar, and leaves on Romeo's orders. Romeo is determined to be with Juliet that night and calls on an Apothecary who can sell him poison.

Think about

• What do you think are the purposes of the detailed description of the Apothecary's shop in lines 37 to 48?

• If you were staging a production set today, what would your Apothecary and his shop look like?

29 **Tush … deceived**: Nonsense, you're mistaken

34 **lie with**: 1 sleep beside; 2 be with as a lover
35 **Let's … means**: How am I going to do it
37 **apothecary**: pharmacist, who makes up medicines
38 **hereabouts 'a dwells**: he lives somewhere around here
   late I noted: I recently spotted
39 **tattered weeds**: ragged clothes
   overwhelming brows: overhanging eyebrows
40 **Culling of simples**: gathering herbs for medicine
   Meagre … looks: He was thin-looking
42 **needy**: poor
45 **beggarly account**: wretchedly small number
46 **bladders**: used as containers for liquids
47 **Remnants of packthread**: bits of string
   cakes of roses: compressed rose petals used as perfume
49 **penury**: poverty
50 **An if**: If
51 **Whose … death**: the sale of which is punishable by immediate execution
52 **caitiff wretch**: wretched creature
53 **forerun**: anticipate
56 **holiday**: a saint's day
59 **ducats**: gold coins

60 **dram**: small quantity
   soon-speeding gear: fast-acting stuff

ROMEO	Tush, thou art deceived.

Leave me, and do the thing I bid thee do.   30
Hast thou no letters to me from the Friar?

BALTHASAR   No, my good lord.

ROMEO   No matter. Get thee gone,
And hire those horses. I'll be with thee straight.

Exit BALTHASAR.

Well, Juliet, I will lie with thee tonight.
Let's see for means. O mischief, thou art swift   35
To enter in the thoughts of desperate men!
I do remember an apothecary,
And hereabouts 'a dwells, which late I noted
In tattered weeds, with overwhelming brows,
Culling of simples. Meagre were his looks.   40
Sharp misery had worn him to the bones.
And in his needy shop a tortoise hung,
An alligator stuffed, and other skins
Of ill-shaped fishes – and about his shelves
A beggarly account of empty boxes,   45
Green earthen pots, bladders, and musty seeds,
Remnants of packthread, and old cakes of roses,
Were thinly scattered to make up a show.
Noting this penury, to myself I said:
'An if a man did need a poison now,   50
Whose sale is present death in Mantua,
Here lives a caitiff wretch would sell it him.'
O, this same thought did but forerun my need –
And this same needy man must sell it me.
As I remember, this should be the house.   55
Being holiday, the beggar's shop is shut.
What ho! Apothecary!

Enter the APOTHECARY.

APOTHECARY   Who calls so loud?

ROMEO   Come hither, man. I see that thou art poor.
Hold, there is forty ducats. (***Showing a bag of gold
coins***) Let me have
A dram of poison – such soon-speeding gear   60

227

The Apothecary is poor and so sells Romeo the deadly poison even though the penalty for doing so is death. Romeo leaves for Verona.

61 disperse: spread

63 trunk ... breath: body will stop breathing
64 hasty powder: explosive gunpowder
65 womb: belly (i.e. interior)
66 mortal: deadly / lethal
67 he: man
utters: makes available / sells
68 bare: poor
69 fear'st: are afraid
70 Need and oppression: i.e. poverty that has ground you down
starveth: produce the effects of hunger
71 Contempt ... back: your clothes show how poor you are, and the way the world despises you for it
73 affords: provides
74 break it: 1 break the law; 2 break out of your poverty

79 dispatch you straight: kill you instantly

82 compounds: mixtures

84 get ... flesh: fatten yourself up

85 cordial: healing medicine

Think about

• Look at what Romeo says to the Apothecary. What is Romeo's attitude to life and the world at this point in the play? How has he changed since the begining of the play?

	As will disperse itself through all the veins,
	That the life-weary taker may fall dead,
	And that the trunk may be discharged of breath
	As violently as hasty powder fired
	Doth hurry from the fatal cannon's womb.

65

APOTHECARY Such mortal drugs I have. But Mantua's law
Is death to any he that utters them.

ROMEO Art thou so bare and full of wretchedness,
And fear'st to die? Famine is in thy cheeks –
Need and oppression starveth in thy eyes, 70
Contempt and beggary hangs upon thy back.
The world is not thy friend, nor the world's law.
The world affords no law to make thee rich –
Then be not poor, but break it, and take this.

APOTHECARY My poverty, but not my will consents. 75

ROMEO I pay thy poverty and not thy will.

APOTHECARY (*Giving him the poison*) Put this in any liquid thing you
will
And drink it off – and if you had the strength
Of twenty men, it would dispatch you straight.

ROMEO (*Giving him the money*) There is thy gold – worse
poison to men's souls, 80
Doing more murder in this loathsome world,
Than these poor compounds that thou mayst not sell.
I sell *thee* poison: thou hast sold me none.
Farewell. Buy food, and get thyself in flesh.

Exit the APOTHECARY.

Come, cordial, and not poison – go with me 85
To Juliet's grave, for there must I use thee.

Exit.

Act 5 Scene 2

In this scene ...

- Friar Lawrence is shocked to hear that Friar John has been unable to deliver his letter to Romeo.
- He rushes off to collect Juliet from the tomb, knowing that she will soon be awake.

Friar John reports to Friar Lawrence that he has been unable to deliver his letter to Romeo. He has been shut up in a house containing people suspected of having the plague.

4 **his mind be writ**: he has written down his thoughts
5 **barefoot brother**: i.e. another Franciscan friar
6 **order**: religious order / community
   associate: accompany
8 **searchers**: city health inspectors
10 **pestilence**: plague
11 **forth**: out
12 **my speed ... stayed**: I was held up there and could not get to Mantua
13 **bare**: delivered
14 **here ... again**: i.e. I have brought it back to you

18 **nice**: trivial / unimportant
    charge: serious matters
19 **Of dear import**: extremely important
21 **crow**: crow-bar
    straight: straight away

Think about

- What does Friar John's explanation tell us about life in Shakespeare's time? Think about friars and their way of life, the plague, and methods of communication. Why are these facts important for the plot?

230

Friar Lawrence's cell.

Enter FRIAR JOHN.

FRIAR JOHN	Holy Franciscan! Friar! Brother, ho!

Enter FRIAR LAWRENCE, *from his inner room.*

FR. LAWRENCE This same should be the voice of Friar John.
Welcome from Mantua! What says Romeo?
Or, if his mind be writ, give me his letter.

FRIAR JOHN Going to find a barefoot brother out, 5
One of our order, to associate me,
Here in this city visiting the sick,
And finding him, the searchers of the town –
Suspecting that we both were in a house
Where the infectious pestilence did reign – 10
Sealed up the doors, and would not let us forth,
So that my speed to Mantua there was stayed.

FR. LAWRENCE Who bare my letter then to Romeo?

FRIAR JOHN I could not send it – here it is again –
Nor get a messenger to bring it thee, 15
So fearful were they of infection.

FR. LAWRENCE Unhappy fortune! By my brotherhood,
The letter was not nice, but full of charge,
Of dear import – and the neglecting it
May do much danger! Friar John, go hence – 20
Get me an iron crow, and bring it straight
Unto my cell.

FRIAR JOHN Brother, I'll go and bring it thee.

Exit.

Friar Lawrence anxiously prepares to break into the Capulet monument, knowing that Juliet is about to wake up. He plans to keep her at his cell until Romeo can collect her.

24 **monument**: tomb

26 **beshrew me much**: be very angry with me
27 **notice ... accidents**: report about what has happened
30 **corse**: corpse

Think about

• Some films represent this scene without dialogue. In the Luhrmann film, a mailman delivers a note to Romeo's caravan which he never finds. In the Zeffirelli film, Balthasar sees Juliet's 'funeral' and gets to Romeo before Friar John does. Do you think these versions are more or less convincing than Shakespeare's?

FR. LAWRENCE Now must I to the monument alone.
Within this three hours will fair Juliet wake.   25
She will beshrew me much that Romeo
Hath had no notice of these accidents.
But I will write again to Mantua,
And keep her at my cell till Romeo come.
Poor living corse, closed in a dead man's tomb!   30

Exit.

In this scene ...

- Romeo kills Paris when he tries to stop him entering the tomb.
- To be with Juliet again, Romeo drinks the poison and dies.
- When the Friar arrives, Juliet wakes up. He tries to hustle her away, but she is determined to stay by Romeo and the Friar flees. Taking Romeo's dagger, Juliet kills herself.
- The Prince, the Capulets and Montague find their children and Paris dead.
- The Friar explains what has happened and the two fathers make peace.

Paris arrives outside the Capulet tomb. When his page signals that someone is coming, he hides.

1 **aloof**: some way off

3 **lay ... along**: lie flat on the ground
4 **hollow**: because of the graves

6 **Being**: i.e. since the soil is
7 **But ... hear**: without you hearing

10 **stand**: stay
11 **adventure**: take the risk

12 **strew**: scatter
13 **canopy**: covering (of her 'bed', the tomb)
14 **sweet water**: perfume
    dew: sprinkle
15 **wanting**: lacking
    distilled by: made out of (like distilled spirits)
16 **obsequies**: funeral rituals

20 **cross**: disturb / interfere with
    rite: rituals

Think about

- How might these opening moments have been staged in Shakespeare's Globe theatre? Think about where Juliet should be placed, where Paris's page should hide, and where Paris should hide.

ACT 5   SCENE 3

Verona: a churchyard, with the family tomb of the Capulets.
Enter Count PARIS *and his* PAGE, *with a torch burning to light*
their way. (The PAGE *brings flowers, and* PARIS *a flask of*
perfumed water.)

PARIS

Give me thy torch, boy. Hence, and stand aloof.
Yet put it out – for I would not be seen.
Under yond yew trees lay thee all along,
Holding thy ear close to the hollow ground –
So shall no foot upon the churchyard tread,   5
Being loose, unfirm with digging up of graves,
But thou shalt hear it. Whistle then to me,
As signal that thou hear'st something approach.
Give me those flowers. Do as I bid thee, go.

PAGE

(*Aside*) I am almost afraid to stand alone   10
Here in the churchyard, yet I will adventure.

The PAGE *moves away and hides.*

PARIS *scatters his flowers and perfumed water at the entrance*
of the tomb, in which JULIET *now lies.*

PARIS

Sweet flower, with flowers thy bridal bed I strew –
O woe, thy canopy is dust and stones! –
Which with sweet water nightly I will dew,
Or, wanting that, with tears distilled by moans.   15
The obsequies that I for thee will keep,
Nightly shall be to strew thy grave and weep.

The PAGE *whistles.*

The boy gives warning! Something doth approach.
What cursèd foot wanders this way tonight,
To cross my obsequies and true love's rite?   20
What, with a torch? Muffle me, night, a while.

PARIS *hides himself near the tomb.*

235

As they enter, Romeo orders Balthasar to leave and not interrupt him, but Balthasar hides nearby. As Romeo tries to get into the tomb, Paris decides to try to arrest him, convinced that he has come to dishonour the bodies lying in the tomb.

22   **mattock**: pick
      wrenching iron: crow-bar
23   **Hold**: Wait
24   **See**: make sure
25   **charge**: order
26   **all aloof**: well out of the way
27   **my course**: what I am doing
28   **Why**: The reason why

32   **In dear employment**: for a very personal purpose
33   **jealous**: suspicious

36   **hungry**: because death has a great appetite
38   **inexorable**: relentless
39   **empty**: hungry

Think about

• Look at lines 23 to 48. What is Romeo thinking and what is he planning to do? Think about why he lies to Balthasar (lines 28 to 32) and speaks so harshly to him.

• What differences do you notice in the way Paris and Romeo speak about the tomb and their purpose in being there? Look at lines 12 to 17, and 45 to 48.

44   **his ... doubt**: I am worried and suspicious about his intentions

45   **maw ... womb**: both can mean 'stomach'

48   **more food**: i.e. Romeo's own body

53   **apprehend**: arrest

Enter ROMEO *and* BALTHASAR, *with a torch burning, carrying a pick and a crow-bar.*

ROMEO	Give me that mattock and the wrenching iron.
	Hold, take this letter. Early in the morning
	See thou deliver it to my lord and father.
	Give me the light. Upon thy life I charge thee,

25

Whate'er thou hear'st or seest, stand all aloof,
And do not interrupt me in my course.
Why I descend into this bed of death
Is partly to behold my lady's face,
But chiefly to take thence from her dead finger   30
A precious ring, a ring that I must use
In dear employment. Therefore hence, be gone.
But if thou, jealous, dost return to pry
In what I farther shall intend to do,
By heaven, I will tear thee joint by joint,   35
And strew this hungry churchyard with thy limbs!
The time and my intents are savage-wild,
More fierce and more inexorable far
Than empty tigers or the roaring sea.

BALTHASAR   I will be gone, sir, and not trouble ye.   40

ROMEO   So shalt thou show me friendship. (*Gives him money*)
        Take thou that.
    Live and be prosperous – and farewell, good fellow.

BALTHASAR   (*Aside*) For all this same, I'll hide me hereabout.
    His looks I fear, and his intents I doubt.

BALTHASAR *goes, but hides further off in the churchyard.* ROMEO *uses the crow-bar to force open the entrance of the tomb.*

ROMEO   Thou detestable maw! – Thou womb of death! –   45
    Gorged with the dearest morsel of the earth! –
    Thus I enforce thy rotten jaws to open,
    And in despite I'll cram thee with more food.

PARIS   (*Aside*) This is that banished haughty Montague
    That murdered my love's cousin, with which grief   50
    It is supposèd the fair creature died –
    And here is come to do some villainous shame
    To the dead bodies. I will apprehend him!

Resisting arrest, Romeo fights Paris and kills him, not knowing who he is. When he recognises the dead man, Romeo grants Paris his dying wish and lays his body next to Juliet's.

54 **unhallowed**: unholy / wicked

58 **therefore ... hither**: that's why I came here
59 **tempt**: provoke
60 **these gone**: i.e. the dead

65 **armed against myself**: i.e. with the poison for my suicide

68 **defy thy conjurations**: reject your wishes and warnings
69 **felon**: criminal

Think about

• The confrontation between Romeo and Paris is cut in both the Zeffirelli and Luhrmann films. What is its purpose? What effect does Romeo killing Paris have on the way we view the story?

• Think about what we learn about Romeo from his reaction to fighting and killing Paris, and the way he treats the dead man.

74 **peruse**: examine / look closely at

76 **betossèd soul**: tormented mind
77 **attend**: listen to
78 **should have**: was supposed to have

82 **writ ... book**: i.e. who shares my unhappy fate

He comes forward to challenge ROMEO.

	Stop thy unhallowed toil, vile Montague!	
	Can vengeance be pursued further than death?	55
	Condemnèd villain, I do apprehend thee!	
	Obey, and go with me, for thou must die.	

ROMEO   I must indeed – and therefore came I hither.
         Good gentle youth, tempt not a desperate man.
         Fly hence and leave me. Think upon these gone –   60
         Let them affright thee. I beseech thee, youth,
         Put not another sin upon my head
         By urging me to fury. O, be gone!
         By heaven, I love thee better than myself
         For I come hither armed against myself.   65
         Stay not, be gone! Live – and hereafter say
         A madman's mercy bid thee run away.

PARIS   (*Drawing his sword*) I do defy thy conjurations
         And apprehend thee for a felon here!

ROMEO   Wilt thou provoke me? Then have at thee, boy!   70

They fight.

PAGE   O Lord, they fight! I will go call the Watch.

Exit, running.

PARIS   (*Falling, mortally wounded*) O, I am slain! If thou be
             merciful,
         Open the tomb. Lay me with Juliet.

He dies.

ROMEO   In faith, I will. Let me peruse this face.
         Mercutio's kinsman, noble County Paris!   75
         What said my man, when my betossèd soul
         Did not attend him as we rode? I think
         He told me Paris should have married Juliet.
         Said he not so? Or did I dream it so?
         Or am I mad, hearing him talk of Juliet,   80
         To think it was so? O, give me thy hand,
         One writ with me in sour misfortune's book!
         I'll bury thee in a triumphant grave. –

Romeo admires Juliet's beauty and, drinking the poison, he kisses her and dies.

84 **lantern**: building designed with many windows to let in light

86 **feasting presence**: chamber for receiving party guests

87 **interred**: buried

89 **keepers**: jailers

90 **lightning**: sudden light-heartedness

92 **honey**: sweetness

94 **ensign**: flag

96 **is not advancèd**: has not reached there yet

99 **cut ... twain**: i.e. killed you when you were young

100 **sunder ... enemy**: i.e. to kill the person who was your enemy (himself)

101 **cousin**: i.e. Tybalt (his cousin by marriage)

103 **unsubstantial**: without a physical body
     amorous: in love

104 **abhorrèd**: revolting / repulsive

105 **paramour**: lover

106 **still**: forever

111 **shake ... stars**: shake off the oppressive weight of my unlucky fortune

115 **dateless bargain**: a contract which will never expire
     engrossing: that consumes everything

116 **conduct**: guide (i.e. the poison)

117 **pilot**: navigator
     run on: run aground on

118 **seasick weary bark**: ship, tired of voyaging (i.e. his body, tired of life)

Think about

- What kind of person does Romeo imagine Death to be in lines 102 to 105?

- Earlier in the play Romeo compared life to a course sailed by a ship (Act 1 Scene 4, lines 113 to 114, and Act 2 Scene 2, lines 82 to 84). How does he develop that idea here? Who is the 'pilot' directing his course (lines 116 to 118)?

He wrenches the tomb-entrance wide open, and drags PARIS's
body inside, where JULIET *already lies.*

          – A grave? – O, no – a lantern, slaughtered youth! –
          For here lies Juliet, and her beauty makes   **85**
          This vault a feasting presence full of light.
          Death, lie thou there, by a dead man interred.

He lays PARIS's *body down, and turns towards* JULIET.

          How oft when men are at the point of death
          Have they been merry, which their keepers call
          A lightning before death! O, how may I   **90**
          Call this a lightning? O my love, my wife!
          Death, that hath sucked the honey of thy breath,
          Hath had no power yet upon thy beauty.
          Thou art not conquered. Beauty's ensign yet
          Is crimson in thy lips and in thy cheeks,   **95**
          And death's pale flag is not advancèd there.
          Tybalt, liest thou there in thy bloody sheet?
          O, what more favour can I do to thee
          Than with that hand that cut thy youth in twain
          To sunder his that was thine enemy?   **100**
          Forgive me, cousin. Ah, dear Juliet,
          Why art thou yet so fair? Shall I believe
          That unsubstantial Death is amorous,
          And that the lean abhorrèd monster keeps
          Thee here in dark to be his paramour?   **105**
          For fear of that I still will stay with thee,
          And never from this palace of dim night
          Depart again. Here, here will I remain,
          With worms that are thy chambermaids. O, here
          Will I set up my everlasting rest,   **110**
          And shake the yoke of inauspicious stars
          From this world-wearied flesh. Eyes, look your last.
          Arms, take your last embrace! – And lips, O you,
          The doors of breath, seal with a righteous kiss
          A dateless bargain to engrossing Death!   **115**
          Come, bitter conduct – come, unsavoury guide! –
          Thou desperate pilot – now at once run on
          The dashing rocks thy seasick weary bark!

Moments too late, Friar Lawrence arrives in the graveyard. Balthasar tells the Friar that Romeo has been in the tomb for some time.

119 apothecary: the person who sold him the poison

120 quick: 1 rapid; 2 lively

121 speed: aid

125 yond: over there
vainly: uselessly

126 discern: make out

127 Capels': Capulets'

132 My master ... but: As far as my master is aware

133 menace: threaten

136 ill unthrifty thing: evil and unlucky happening

Think about

- In the text, Juliet wakes just after Romeo's death. In the Luhrmann film, he remains alive just long enough to realise that Juliet is not dead and then she sees him die. Which version do you prefer and why?

Here's to my love! (*Drinks the poison*) O true
 apothecary!
Thy drugs are quick. Thus with a kiss I die.   **120**

He dies, falling beside JULIET.

Enter FRIAR LAWRENCE, *in the churchyard, with a lantern,
crow-bar and spade.*

FR. LAWRENCE Saint Francis be my speed! How oft tonight
      Have my old feet stumbled at graves! Who's there?

BALTHASAR (*Coming forward*) Here's one, a friend, and one that
     knows you well.

FR. LAWRENCE Bliss be upon you! Tell me, good my friend,
      What torch is yond that vainly lends his light   **125**
      To grubs and eyeless skulls? As I discern
      It burneth in the Capels' monument.

BALTHASAR It doth so, holy sir – and there's my master,
     One that you love.

FR. LAWRENCE   Who is it?

BALTHASAR   Romeo.

FR. LAWRENCE How long hath he been there?

BALTHASAR   Full half an hour.   **130**

FR. LAWRENCE Go with me to the vault.

BALTHASAR   I dare not, sir.
     My master knows not but I am gone hence,
     And fearfully did menace me with death
     If I did stay to look on his intents.

FR. LAWRENCE Stay then – I'll go alone. Fear comes upon me.   **135**
      O, much I fear some ill unthrifty thing!

BALTHASAR As I did sleep under this yew tree here,
     I dreamt my master and another fought,
     And that my master slew him.

Anxious when he sees blood on the ground, Friar Lawrence enters the tomb. As he finds the bodies of Romeo and Paris, Juliet awakes and asks him where Romeo is. He tries to explain, but, hearing voices approaching, wants to hurry her away. When she realises that Romeo is dead, she refuses to go. Friar Lawrence flees without her.

141   **sepulchre**: tomb
142   **masterless**: abandoned by their owners
      gory: bloody

145   **unkind**: cruel and unnatural
146   **guilty … chance**: responsible for this tragic happening

148   **comfortable**: comforting / reassuring

152   **contagion**: disease
153   **contradict**: argue against
154   **thwarted our intents**: prevented us from doing what we wanted to do
155   **thy bosom**: your arms
156–7 **dispose … Among**: find you a place with

162   **timeless**: 1 everlasting; 2 untimely
163   **churl**: ill-mannered person
164   **after**: come after / follow
165   **Haply**: Perhaps
166   **restorative**: 1 cure; 2 something to restore her to him

---

Think about

• Actor Niamh Cusack played the moment when Juliet wakes very happily: she believed that everything had gone to plan. What effect might a happy Juliet at that moment have on the audience?

• What is your opinion of the Friar's words and behaviour after Juliet awakes? What do you think of his suggestions to Juliet? Is he right to run away?

244

FR. LAWRENCE   Romeo! –
                     (*Approaching the tomb, and stooping to examine the
                        ground*) – Alack, alack! – What blood is this which
                        stains   140
                     The stony entrance of this sepulchre?
                     What mean these masterless and gory swords
                     To lie discoloured by this place of peace?

He enters the tomb.

                     Romeo! O pale! Who else? What, Paris too? –
                     And steeped in blood? Ah, what an unkind hour   145
                     Is guilty of this lamentable chance!

JULIET *wakes, and begins to sit up.*

                     The lady stirs.

JULIET   O comfortable Friar! – Where is my lord?
                     I do remember well where I should be,
                     And there I am. Where is my Romeo?   150

Voices are heard in the churchyard.

FR. LAWRENCE I hear some noise, lady. Come from that nest
                     Of death, contagion, and unnatural sleep.
                     A greater power than we can contradict
                     Hath thwarted our intents. Come, come away!
                     Thy husband in thy bosom there lies dead –   155
                     And Paris too. Come, I'll dispose of thee
                     Among a sisterhood of holy nuns.
                     Stay not to question, for the Watch is coming.
                     Come, go, good Juliet! – I dare no longer stay.

JULIET   Go, get thee hence – for I will not away.   160

                                        Exit FRIAR LAWRENCE.

                     What's here? A cup closed in my true love's hand?
                     Poison, I see, hath been his timeless end.
                     O churl! – drunk all, and left no friendly drop
                     To help me after? I will kiss thy lips.
                     Haply some poison yet doth hang on them   165
                     To make me die with a restorative.
                     (*Kissing him*) Thy lips are warm.

Juliet kills herself with Romeo's dagger. The Watchmen enter the tomb and discover the bodies. As the Friar and Balthasar are detained and brought in, the Prince arrives.

169 **brief**: quick
     happy: found at the right time

170 **This**: i.e. her breast

173 **attach**: arrest

179 **woes**: miserable creatures (i.e. the three dead bodies)
180 **ground**: 1 underlying reason for; 2 earth (wordplay)
     woes: unhappy events
181 **cannot … descry**: cannot discover without further details
183 **in safety**: securely

185 **mattock**: pick

187 **A great suspicion**: That looks extremely suspicious
     Stay: Hold

Think about

• What purposes do the Watchmen fulfil here? What are the arguments for and against cutting their dialogue (lines 171 to 201) and having no gap between Juliet's death and the entrance of the main characters, who could all begin to arrive at line 202?

Enter Paris's PAGE, with the men of the WATCH, approaching the tomb.

WATCHMAN 1 Lead, boy. Which way?

JULIET Yea, noise? Then I'll be brief! –
(She snatches Romeo's dagger from his belt.)
O happy dagger!
This is thy sheath! *(Stabbing herself)* – There rust, and
let me die.   170

She falls across ROMEO's body, and dies.

PAGE This is the place – there, where the torch doth burn!

WATCHMAN 1 The ground is bloody. Search about the churchyard.
Go, some of you. Whoe'er you find, attach.

WATCHMEN go out searching.

The FIRST WATCHMAN enters the tomb, then comes out again.

Pitiful sight! Here lies the County slain,
And Juliet bleeding, warm and newly dead,   175
Who here hath lain this two days burièd!
Go, tell the Prince, run to the Capulets!
Raise up the Montagues! Some others search.

More WATCHMEN go off.

We see the ground whereon these woes do lie,
But the true ground of all these piteous woes   180
We cannot without circumstance descry.

Re-enter a WATCHMAN, bringing BALTHASAR.

WATCHMAN 2 Here's Romeo's man. We found him in the churchyard.

WATCHMAN 1 Hold him in safety till the Prince come hither.

Re-enter another WATCHMAN, with FRIAR LAWRENCE.

WATCHMAN 3 Here is a Friar that trembles, sighs, and weeps.
We took this mattock and this spade from him,   185
As he was coming from this churchyard's side.

WATCHMAN 1 A great suspicion! Stay the Friar too.

Juliet's parents arrive and find their daughter dead. Montague arrives and sadly reports that his wife has died from grief at Romeo's banishment. He is stunned to find his son dead in the tomb.

—Think about—

• The Prince's wordplay with Montague (lines 208 to 209) can seem inappropriate at such a sad moment, yet Montague himself plays with imagery (lines 214 to 215). What effect does wordplay have at this point?

188 **misadventure ... up**: dreadful event has happened so early in the day

190 **shrieked abroad**: screamed out in the streets

194 **fear ... ears**: is this fearful event you are hearing about

200 **instruments**: tools

203 **has mista'en**: is in the wrong place
house: sheath
204 **Montague**: i.e. Romeo

207 **warns ... sepulchre**: summons me to my grave

209 **more early down**: already dead
210 **liege**: sovereign
is dead to-night: died during the night

214 **thou untaught**: you ill-mannered boy

215 **press before**: push in front of

Enter PRINCE ESCALUS, *with attendants.*

PRINCE   What misadventure is so early up,
                That calls our person from our morning rest?

Enter CAPULET, *and* LADY CAPULET.

CAPULET   What should it be that is so shrieked abroad?   **190**

LADY CAPULET   The people in the streets cry 'Romeo!' –
                Some 'Juliet!', and some 'Paris!', and all run
                With open outcry toward our monument.

PRINCE   What fear is this which startles in your ears?

WATCHMAN 1   Sovereign, here lies the County Paris slain;   **195**
                And Romeo dead; and Juliet, dead before –
                Warm and new killed.

PRINCE   Search, seek, and know how this foul murder comes!

WATCHMAN 1   Here is a Friar, and slaughtered Romeo's man,
                With instruments upon them fit to open   **200**
                These dead men's tombs.

CAPULET   (*Seeing the bodies*) O heavens! O wife, look how our
                    daughter bleeds!
                This dagger has mista'en, for lo, his house
                Is empty on the back of Montague,
                And is mis-sheathèd in my daughter's bosom.   **205**

LADY CAPULET   O me! This sight of death is as a bell
                That warns my old age to a sepulchre!

Enter MONTAGUE, *with servants.*

PRINCE   Come, Montague – for thou art early up
                To see thy son and heir more early down.

MONTAGUE   Alas, my liege, my wife is dead tonight.   **210**
                Grief of my son's exile hath stopped her breath.
                What further woe conspires against mine age?

PRINCE   Look, and thou shalt see.

MONTAGUE   (*Seeing* ROMEO's *body*) O thou untaught! What
                    manners is in this,
                To press before thy father to a grave?   **215**

Friar Lawrence tells what he knows about the events that have led to the tragic deaths.

216 Seal ... outrage: Stop your expressions of passionate grief

217 clear ... ambiguities: clear up these mysteries

218 spring ... descent: origin, cause and true sequence of events

219 be ... woes: lead you in mourning

220 even to death: i.e. the death of the guilty
forbear: control your feelings

221 let mischance ... patience: allow your patience to keep a hold on your misfortunes

222 parties of suspicion: suspects

223 the greatest: most liable to be suspected

225 Doth ... me: throws suspicion on me
direful: terrible

226–7 impeach ... excused: accuse myself and be found guilty, and to make excuses and be pardoned

228 in: of

229 date of breath: time I have to live

233 stol'n: secret

234 doomsday: day of death

237 remove ... her: relieve her of the grief possessing her

238 Betrothed: promised her in marriage
perforce: forcibly

240 devise some mean: think up some way

243 tutored by my art: guided by my special knowledge

245–6 wrought ... form: gave her the appearance

247 as: on
dire: terrible

248 borrowed: temporary

249 force should cease: effect should wear off

251 stayed: delayed

Think about

• As the audience has already seen the events the Friar describes, what purpose does his speech serve?

• How would you direct the other main characters to behave during the Friar's speech?

PRINCE	Seal up the mouth of outrage for a while,
	Till we can clear these ambiguities –
	And know their spring, their head, their true descent.
	And then will I be general of your woes,
	And lead you even to death. Meantime forbear,	220
	And let mischance be slave to patience.
	Bring forth the parties of suspicion.

FRIAR LAWRENCE *and* BALTHASAR *are brought forward.*

FR. LAWRENCE	I am the greatest – able to do least,
	Yet most suspected, as the time and place
	Doth make against me, of this direful murder.	225
	And here I stand, both to impeach and purge,
	Myself condemnèd and myself excused.

| PRINCE | Then say at once what thou dost know in this. |

FR. LAWRENCE	I will be brief, for my short date of breath
	Is not so long as is a tedious tale.	230
	Romeo, there dead, was husband to that Juliet –
	And she, there dead, that Romeo's faithful wife.
	I married them. And their stol'n marriage day
	Was Tybalt's doomsday, whose untimely death
	Banished the new-made bridegroom from this city –	235
	For whom, and not for Tybalt, Juliet pined.
	You, to remove that siege of grief from her,
	Betrothed and would have married her perforce
	To County Paris. Then comes she to me,
	And with wild looks bid me devise some mean	240
	To rid her from this second marriage –
	Or in my cell there would she kill herself.
	Then gave I her, so tutored by my art,
	A sleeping potion, which so took effect
	As I intended, for it wrought on her	245
	The form of death. Meantime I writ to Romeo
	That he should hither come as this dire night
	To help to take her from her borrowed grave,
	Being the time the potion's force should cease.
	But he which bore my letter, Friar John,	250
	Was stayed by accident, and yesternight
	Returned my letter back. Then all alone,

251

Balthasar and Paris's page also tell the Prince what they know.

253 **prefixèd**: pre-arranged

255 **closely**: secretly

257 **ere**: before

260 **entreated**: begged

266 **is privy**: shares the secret
     aught: anything
267 **Miscarried**: went wrong
268 **hour ... time**: time before I might have been expected to die
269 **Unto ... law**: in line with the strictest interpretation of the law
270 **still**: always
273 **post**: a great hurry

275 **early**: as soon as I could
276 **going in**: as he was going into
277 **If I departed not**: unless I went away

---Think about---

• There are other points in the play where characters report what has happened. Look at Act 3 Scene 1, lines 148 to 171, and Act 5 Scene 3, lines 137 to 139. How are these reports different from the Friar's? Think about the way they describe the events they have been involved in.

280 **made your master**: was your master doing
282 **aloof**: out of the way
283 **Anon**: Straight afterwards
284 **by and by**: almost at once

286 **make ... words**: back up what the Friar said

At the prefixèd hour of her waking,
Came I to take her from her kindred's vault –
Meaning to keep her closely at my cell   255
Till I conveniently could send to Romeo.
But when I came, some minute ere the time
Of her awakening, here untimely lay
The noble Paris and true Romeo dead.
She wakes – and I entreated her come forth   260
And bear this work of heaven with patience.
But then a noise did scare me from the tomb,
And she, too desperate, would not go with me –
But, as it seems, did violence on herself.
All this I know, and to the marriage   265
Her Nurse is privy. And if aught in this
Miscarried by my fault, let my old life
Be sacrificed some hour before his time
Unto the rigour of severest law.

PRINCE   We still have known thee for a holy man.   270
                Where's Romeo's man? What can he say to this?

BALTHASAR   I brought my master news of Juliet's death,
                And then in post he came from Mantua
                To this same place, to this same monument.
                This letter he early bid me give his father, 275
                And threatened me with death, going in the vault,
                If I departed not and left him there.

PRINCE   Give me the letter. I will look on it.
                Where is the County's page that raised the watch?

The PAGE *comes forward.*

                Sirrah, what made your master in this place?   280

PAGE   He came with flowers to strew his lady's grave,
                And bid me stand aloof, and so I did.
                Anon comes one with light to ope the tomb,
                And by and by my master drew on him,
                And then I ran away to call the Watch.   285

PRINCE   This letter doth make good the Friar's words,
                Their course of love, the tidings of her death.
                And here he writes that he did buy a poison

The Prince summons the two fathers to look at the terrible results of their hatred. Montague and Capulet make peace, each one promising to set up a golden statue as a monument to the other man's child. The Prince declares that some people will be punished and some pardoned, and concludes the story of Romeo and Juliet.

289 therewithal: i.e. with the poison
292 scourge: i.e. punishment
293 kill ... love: i.e. use love to kill your children
294 winking ... discords: shutting my eyes to your quarrels
295 brace: pair (i.e. Mercutio and Paris)
297 jointure: marriage-settlement (the dowry which the father of the bride would be expected to pay)

301 figure: statue / image
at such ... set: be valued so highly

304 Poor sacrifices of: 1 sad victims of; 2 inadequate compensation / payment for
enmity: hatred
305 glooming: cloudy

Think about

- The Prince says that some will be pardoned and some punished. Who do you think should be pardoned, and who punished?

- Will there now be peace or will the feud start up again, in your opinion? In what different ways could you stage the ending to bring out these contrasting interpretations?

	Of a poor 'pothecary, and therewithal	
	Came to this vault, to die and lie with Juliet.	290
	Where be these enemies? Capulet, Montague?	
	See what a scourge is laid upon your hate,	
	That heaven finds means to kill your joys with love!	
	And I, for winking at your discords too,	
	Have lost a brace of kinsmen. All are punished.	295
CAPULET	O brother Montague, give me thy hand.	
	This is my daughter's jointure – for no more	
	Can I demand.	
MONTAGUE	But I can give thee more –	
	For I will raise her statue in pure gold,	
	That whiles Verona by that name is known,	300
	There shall no figure at such rate be set	
	As that of true and faithful Juliet.	
CAPULET	As rich shall Romeo's by his lady's lie –	
	Poor sacrifices of our enmity!	
PRINCE	A glooming peace this morning with it brings.	305
	The sun for sorrow will not show his head.	
	Go hence, to have more talk of these sad things.	
	Some shall be pardoned, and some punishèd.	
	– For never was a story of more woe	
	Than this of Juliet and her Romeo.	310

Exeunt.

Shakespeare's Globe, 2004

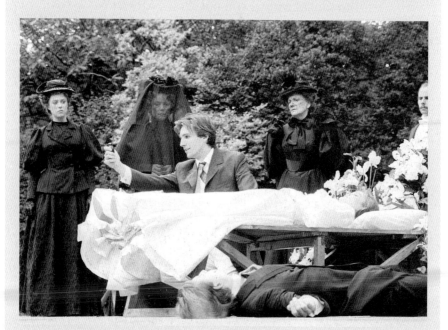

Open Air Theatre, Regent's Park, 1986

National Theatre, 2000

Romeo and Juliet, 1996 (directed by B. Luhrmann)

RSC, 1986

RSC, 1989

259

We do not know exactly when Shakespeare wrote *Romeo and Juliet*, but it was probably around 1595. He did not invent the story of the two young lovers; it had been popular throughout Europe for fifty years. But Shakespeare did convert it into a tragedy about love, honour and fate, which remains one of his most popular plays.

LOVE AND COURTSHIP

In Shakespeare's time it was not always possible for a girl and boy simply to fall in love and get married. Wealthy families, like the Capulets, would arrange marriages for their children for any number of reasons that had nothing to do with love. They might want their child to marry into a wealthy family, for example, or into one with a noble title like Count Paris's.

Courtship in powerful or noble families followed certain rules. Paris has to ask Juliet's father for permission to woo her. Fathers were especially powerful figures and their children were expected to do as they were told. In England the law said that a daughter was legally her father's property until she got married, when she became the property of her husband. Capulet is confident that Juliet will be 'ruled in all respects' by him and seems to think that he can give her away to whichever husband he chooses.

HONOUR

An individual's personal pride and reputation were extremely important as a person would feel very proud to have a famous and respected family name, such as Capulet or Montague. If one family felt insulted or injured by another, they might seek revenge, and a family feud would have begun which could continue for generations. Shakespeare's audience would have associated Italy, where the story is set, with violent passions: a place where a strong sense of family honour could often lead to violent acts of revenge and feuds.

When Tybalt finally meets up with Romeo, he calls him a 'villain'. In Shakespeare's time, this was an insult to a man's birth and his behaviour. It suggested that he was both low-born and of bad character. It would be enough to provoke a duel, which is what Tybalt wants. Mercutio, who also understands the code of honour, cannot understand or tolerate Romeo's refusal to take up the challenge. When Mercutio is killed, Romeo feels ashamed, and his sense of honour tells him that it is his duty to get revenge for his friend's death.

FATE

Romeo and Juliet are described in the Prologue as 'star-crossed lovers'. This means that their love is doomed not to succeed. Shakespeare's audience would have understood the idea that fate controlled people's lives and would have noticed all the references in the play to 'the stars'. For audiences today, Romeo and Juliet's tragedy seems more a case of simple bad luck. The young lovers certainly do seem to have their share of ill fortune, and a lot of it is to do with unlucky timing. It is particularly unfortunate, for example, that the Friar arrives at the tomb only seconds after Romeo has drunk the poison. It is as though, whatever Romeo and Juliet do, the course of their lives is already written in the stars. Their love is 'death-marked' and they cannot avoid their fate.

TRAGEDY

A tragedy is a play that shows how a happy and successful person suffers a great disaster that ends in their death. The audience knows from the Prologue that Romeo and Juliet will die at the end of this particular tragedy. In a tragedy the hero's or heroine's destruction might be caused by fate, or by a weakness in the person's character, or by a combination of the two. Romeo and Juliet's tragedy is mainly to do with fate. They are victims of the hatred between their two families and a series of unlucky events that lead to their deaths.

THEATRES AND STAGES

Romeo and Juliet was probably first performed in the mid-1590s, in the playhouse simply called The Theatre, in Shoreditch, on what was then the north-east edge of London. Later performances took place at the Curtain, another theatre nearby, before Shakespeare's acting company (known then as the Lord Chamberlain's Men) finally moved to its new home at the Globe playhouse in 1599.

The earlier playhouses were theatres of the same familiar type as the more famous Globe. The Theatre, in fact, was pulled down and its timbers re-used for building the Globe, so the size of the stage, and the yard and galleries round it, were probably much the same. A performance of *Romeo and Juliet* in a reconstruction of the Curtain playhouse was featured in the film *Shakespeare in Love* (1998).

What we know about the early staging of *Romeo and Juliet* comes mainly from the action of the play itself and the evidence of its stage directions. Three features are most important: the continuous and varying use of the large main-stage platform; the famous 'balcony' or 'window' scenes involving the lovers acting 'aloft', as the old directions say; and the need for some special stagings, such as Juliet's curtained bed (on which she collapses apparently dead in Act 4), and the tomb or 'monument' of the Capulets (for the climax of the tragedy in Act 5).

ACTION AND SETTINGS

The action of the play in an Elizabethan theatre would have been fast and continuous, with no intervals between Acts or Scenes. New scenes are often marked simply by the entrance of new characters. When the Capulet servants hurry in to clear up in Act 1 Scene 5, for example, they show that we are now 'indoors' for the dance at which Romeo and Juliet will meet – even though the visiting maskers who were 'outside' before had remained on the stage. No scenery or stage-lighting, as we think of them, were used. The play's language and activity were enough to suggest places and settings to the imagination of its audience. Burning torches, used several times in *Romeo and Juliet*, were not for lighting, but to tell the audience, in the open-air afternoon daylight of an Elizabethan theatre, that it was watching a 'night-time' scene.

Costumes (indoor or outdoor dress, expensive or 'poor') would also have signalled different settings and different kinds of character for spectators. Montague and Capulet servants, for example, might well have worn different coloured 'uniforms', or badges to represent their family. Balthasar, in Act 5 Scene 1, enters wearing riding-boots as a signal that he has just ridden hurriedly from Verona, and the Apothecary, in the same scene, wears 'tattered' clothes to show his poverty, in sharp contrast with the expensively fashionable dress that most main characters would have worn.

Some changes of setting in Romeo and Juliet can seem odd or complicated. Act 2 Scene 1 begins, for instance, with Romeo hiding himself from Mercutio and Benvolio as they leave the dance. He does this, we are told, by climbing a wall into the garden or 'orchard' of the Capulet house, though he still overhears Mercutio's rude attempts to 'conjure him up'. When he comes out of his hiding-place a new scene begins, continuing straight on from the last, and he is *inside* the garden, 'in darkness', and will see Juliet appear above at her 'window'. On the stage there would almost certainly have been no 'wall' to climb: Romeo may well simply have scrambled behind one of the oak pillars that held up the canopy over the stage. When he emerges, the stage-setting has changed, but *only* in the imagination of the audience, from 'street' to private 'garden', and the stage-pillar may now seem to represent a tree.

When Romeo leaves Juliet after their night together, in Act 3 Scene 5, he climbs down the rope-ladder from her window and departs, again, through the garden. Juliet then comes quickly down herself ('*She goeth down from the window*', the old direction says – but not of course by the rope-ladder). She enters below, to meet her mother and hear the bad news that she is to be married to Paris. The main stage, which was the 'garden', is now only another part of her bedroom: one modern director remarked that she 'brings her bedroom downstairs with her'. The change depends, again, on the imagination of the audience. Characters and their words and behaviour tell us where they are. Juliet's parents, we imagine, invade her bedroom: they are not, of course, likely to have furious family arguments in the garden.

WINDOWS AND DISCOVERIES

As in the Globe playhouse, there would have been two main entrances to the stage from the dressing-room area behind it. Between them, centrally positioned, would have been another opening, usually covered by curtains. This was known as the 'discovery space', because special items, such as a bed or a tomb in *Romeo and Juliet*, could be pushed out through it or revealed ('discovered') inside it. Above this, on the back-wall of the stage (probably about three metres up) would have been the railed upper gallery, which would have served as Juliet's window or balcony, reached by a stairway behind the stage-wall. Juliet would have come down this in Act 3 Scene 5 to re-enter on the stage below.

All we can be sure of, however Juliet's bed or the Capulet tomb was staged, is that they would have had to be visible to spectators on three sides of the stage. Juliet's bed may have been inside the discovery space, or a curtained four-poster bed may have been pushed out. The Capulet tomb, in Act 5, is more of a 'special effect'. Romeo must break open its doors or gates to reach Juliet inside it, and action around and inside it during the final scene of the tragedy must also have been easy enough for spectators to see. In this case, perhaps, the 'monument' may have been a specially built structure pushed forward from the discovery space. Around the monument, the main-stage 'graveyard' would have been in full use, with characters hiding, fighting, arriving too late, and then crowding to see 'this sight of death'.

DEMANDS, FIGHTS AND DOUBLES

Romeo and Juliet would certainly have been a challenging play for Shakespeare's company to put on. We know, for example, that audiences were keen fans of good sword fighting and several fast and thrilling fights (like the one that leads to Mercutio's death in Act 3 Scene 1) would have had to be skilfully managed.

The play also has more than thirty speaking parts. Yet the acting company, including the specialist boy-actors who took female parts (though Juliet's Nurse would have been a man), would have had no more than twelve to fourteen players. Parts therefore had to be 'doubled', which was usual enough in the Elizabethan theatre. Benvolio, for instance, may be missing from the end of the play because the actor who played him has taken on another role. There would certainly have been other minor roles for the actors who played Mercutio and Tybalt to play after their 'deaths' in Act 3. Some players may well have had three or four of the smaller parts. This would have been managed effectively by using changes of costume, and sometimes also by changing appearance with wigs and beards.

Staging in Shakespeare's theatre may seem crude or simple by modern standards, but it was extremely flexible and effective in playing to the imaginations of its audiences. And *Romeo and Juliet* had all the ingredients, of language (from fine poetry to rapid wit and dirty jokes) and of action (the thrills of young love, danger and death), to make it a theatrical success.

A play in performance at the reconstruction of Shakespeare's Globe

Romeo and Juliet is one of Shakespeare's most popular plays. Audiences have always been moved and inspired by the tragedy of the two lovers, perhaps because they are so young, and because their deaths seem such a terrible waste. Modern audiences, however, take a different view of the lovers' story from audiences of Shakespeare's time. Most people today, for example, don't believe that our lives are ruled by fate or that the future is written in the stars.

It also seems likely that Shakespeare's audiences would have sympathised much more with Juliet's parents than many modern audiences do because they expected parents to have complete authority over their children. In the poem by Arthur Brooke on which Shakespeare based his play, the young lovers are condemned for their disobedience and their deaths are partly seen as a punishment for their sins. Modern audiences will also be divided over the issue of arranged marriages. Many people will take the view that Romeo and Juliet have every right to choose who they want to marry, sympathising with them rather than with the parents.

As a result of these issues there are some basic questions that any modern director of this play has to address. Three of the most important are:
- Who or what is to blame for Romeo and Juliet's deaths?
- Who should we sympathise with?
- What time and place should the play be set in to get the chosen interpretation across to the audience?

WHO IS TO BLAME?
Hardly any modern productions take the view that Romeo and Juliet are responsible for their own downfall because of some weakness in their characters. And, as most people no longer believe in astrology or fate, stage and screen interpretations tend not to place all the blame on 'the stars' either. Instead, responsibility for the deaths is usually laid upon other characters, or upon the society in which the young lovers have grown up.

Baz Luhrmann's 1996 film (pages 8, 10, 12, 14, 74, 104, 147, 257) places the lovers in a world in which order has completely broken down. 'Captain Prince' seems powerless to stop the violent rioting in the city's streets and can do little more than observe the chaos from a police helicopter. In this modern version of the story all the men carry guns (decorated with the Capulet or Montague badge) and use them with deadly accuracy. The message seems to be that, in a society such as this, young men like Romeo have little chance of avoiding violence.

Michael Bogdanov took a similar view in his 1986 RSC production set in modern-day Italy (pages 13, 15, 126, 146). Capulet was a mafia boss who had little interest in his daughter except as a way of extending his business empire. Bogdanov chose to end the play with a sort of press conference for the two fathers. Newspaper photographers rushed on to take their photographs as they posed, shaking hands, in front of an enormous gold statue of their dead children. The two fathers were not really affected by their children's deaths, but were using them as an opportunity for a business merger between their two 'companies', Capulet and Montague.

Romeo and Juliet, 1996 (directed by B. Luhrmann)

WHO DO WE SYMPATHISE WITH?

Directors also have to decide who they want the audience to sympathise with. Should their sympathy be only for the younger characters? Or should they have some for the older generation as well?

Franco Zeffirelli's 1968 film shows Romeo and Juliet as two sincere and innocent young people suffering because of their parents' inflexible attitudes. The Capulets only seem concerned with carrying on the feud and have little time for their children. In this version the audience feels hardly any sympathy for the older generation. Only the Friar seems to be good-hearted in trying his best to bring the families together.

Baz Luhrmann is even harder on the adults. In his 1996 film Juliet's parents are selfish, heavy-drinking drug-takers, much more interested in throwing a glamorous party than in caring for their daughter. The Friar, while trying to be in touch with the young people under his care, seems to give up when he realises that Romeo has not received his letter and does not even go to the tomb to take care of the waking Juliet.

One version that did show some sympathy for the parents was the **BBC Television** production first shown in 1978 and available on video. This concentrated much more on the family relationships, using effective camera close-ups to show the characters' feelings, and was especially sympathetic to Capulet. The old man seemed bewildered by the events around him and uncertain about how to cope with a headstrong young daughter.

Romeo and Juliet, 1968 (directed by F. Zeffirelli)

THE SETTING

Productions of Romeo and Juliet have set the play in every period from the fifteenth century to the twenty-first, and in places as different as medieval Verona in Italy and modern-day 'Verona Beach' in the USA.

Zeffirelli's 1968 film chose to set the story in the time and place in which it is supposed to have taken place: fifteenth century Verona. This gave an opportunity to show some dramatic sword fights set in authentic medieval city streets and characters dressed in brilliantly coloured costumes: the Montagues wore blue-green, the Capulets red and yellow. The historical setting helped the audience to understand, for example, how someone banished from the city would be difficult to contact and how the crucial letter from the Friar could so easily fail to reach Romeo.

Two key interpretations, however, have chosen a modern setting: the 1996 **Baz Luhrmann** film and **Michael Bogdanov**'s 1986 RSC production. A modern setting has the obvious attraction that it can speak directly to today's audience, and both of these productions were extremely popular with teenagers. In the 1986 RSC version Tybalt arrived on stage driving a red convertible and the fight started when the aerial was snapped off his car for use as a weapon. Romeo was played as something of an outsider in a group of friends who were constantly trying to impress each other. The Luhrmann film opened with shots of street-rioting and an American city skyline dominated by a gigantic statue of Christ and two towering skyscrapers housing the headquarters of the Montague and Capulet empires. A modern setting like this can help us to understand how a Friar could have been such an important and influential figure in fifteenth century Verona. He was played as a tough city priest and it was easy to see why the teenagers would be influenced by him. His huge statue-topped church showed why he would also have such power and status with their parents.

The activities in this section focus on different scenes in the play. The types of activity used can easily be adapted to focus on other sections of the play if necessary. Before beginning the activities you will need to have read the relevant scene.

ACT 1 SCENE 1: THE OPENING OF THE PLAY

Each activity in this section leads directly onto the next. However, it is possible to use any of them separately. The focus of the activities is on the world of Verona and the feud.

THE WORLD OF THE PLAY

This scene sets up the world of the play: the physical environment, society and atmosphere. It is a place where passion is very important and where people are motivated by aggression and desire.

1 a In pairs read through the scene and make notes on what you think Verona is like. For example, you could consider the following:

- What is the weather like?
- Is it a busy place?
- Does it feel safe on the streets? Why?
- How does it operate politically? Who is in charge? How do they rule?
- Is there a gap between the young and the old? Who has control? How?

   b If you were designing a set for Verona, what would it look like? You could look at the set photographs on pages 258 and 259 to see some examples. Consider:

- How could you show the effects of the feud? In some productions, for example, the fighting has led to the destruction of statues or even buildings. In others it has created borders where different areas of Verona have become 'territory' for one family or the other.
- Would there be lots of hiding places?
- Would it be light or dark? What colours would you use?
- How would you get across the feeling of heat to the audience?

2 a In pairs imagine that one of you is a Capulet and the other is a Montague. You were both at the brawl which begins the play. Think about exactly what happened to you. You could consider the following:

  - Why were you in the street? Where were you going?
  - What can you see if you look around? What sounds can you hear?
  - When and how did you first know there was trouble?
  - What action did you take and were you injured?
  - How did you feel when the Prince arrived and stopped the fight?

  b Take turns to tell your story to your partner. Make sure that you tell the story as if it happened to you. The listener should then ask questions.

3 a In pairs consider the kinds of attitudes that exist in a society that has been at war for a long time, particularly a civil war.

  Examples
  The culture of revenge – an eye for an eye
  Acceptance of violence

  b With your partner discuss in what ways the young people in such a society would be affected. Do you think that young people would grow up quickly in a place like this?

  c One of you should be a young Montague, the other a young Capulet. Devise a short scene in which you meet on the streets after a fight has taken place. It is a hot afternoon, the time when most of the trouble happens. Consider:

  - What do each of the characters expect to happen?
  - What do they want to happen?
  - Do the two characters fight?
  - If not, what stops them?

  d As a group discuss what the scenes show about attitudes towards the feud.

ATTITUDES TOWARDS THE FEUD

1 a In pairs read through Act 1 Scene 1. Make a list of the different attitudes towards the fighting held by the different characters: Sampson, Gregory, Abraham, Benvolio, Tybalt, Capulet, Lady Capulet, Montague, Lady Montague, the Prince and Romeo.

b Find a quotation that shows how each character feels about the feud and write a line in your own words, summarising their view.

Example

TYBALT   What, drawn, and talk of peace? I hate the word
As I hate hell, all Montagues, and thee.
I'll never rest until the Montague scum are destroyed.

2 a In groups of ten make a freeze-frame of the moment when the Prince enters. The characters are the Prince, Gregory, Sampson, Abraham, Tybalt, Benvolio, Capulet, Lady Capulet, Montague and Lady Montague. Each character should speak their thought at the moment that the fighting is stopped by the Prince.

b Each take one of the characters above and write a short speech for them. Imagine it is later that evening and your character is telling a friend about the Prince's new ruling. Consider:

- Does your character think that this is too harsh, or necessary in order to restore peace to the city?
- Do they think it will be effective in stopping the feud?

LOVE

The play shows many different kinds of love and different attitudes towards love and desire. The first is Sampson's boast that he will 'thrust his maids to the wall', meaning that he will have sex with any Montague woman he encounters. This links together sex and violence from the beginning of the play. The idea of courtly love saw love as a sickness which the lover suffered from, and this can be seen in Romeo who is pining for Rosaline.

1 In pairs read from line 154 to the end of scene. Make a list of ten ways in which Romeo thinks he is suffering.

Example
The time goes so slowly when you are in love.

2 Discuss how far the audience should feel that Romeo is really in love at the end of this scene. Does Romeo's suffering convince either the other characters or the audience that his feelings are genuine?

ACT 1 SCENE 5: THE BALL

Each activity in this section leads directly onto the next. However, it is possible to use any of them separately. The focus of the activities is on the juxtaposition of love and hate at the Capulet feast.

PARTY

1   The Capulet ball can be staged in many different ways. In some productions the first section between the servants is cut. In pairs imagine that you are staging a production and have decided to include this section. Consider:

   • How could you use this to create a sense of urgency and pace, and therefore tension, for the coming scene?
   • How could it establish the wealth and splendour, and therefore status, of the Capulets?

2   a   In pairs imagine that you are directing and designing the production. Consider:

   • How would you decorate the stage for the ball?
   • How would you dress the characters?
   • What kinds of masks would you use? Would only the men be wearing them, as was the custom at the time?
   • How many guests would you have?
   • What style of music and dancing would you use?
   • Where would you place the characters to ensure that the audience's focus stays on the main characters?

   b   Draw a sketch or picture of one moment that you think captures the essence of the ball. Use it to show the set design as well as the character's positions. Give each character you have drawn a line of speech from the play or a thought bubble. For example, if you choose the moment when Romeo enters the house, you might decide his thought is 'Where's Rosaline?'.

LOVE

The moment when Romeo and Juliet meet at the ball is a famous example of love at first sight, but it is not easy to stage. It is a significant moment of change and for this to be convincing to the audience it is important to show, when they enter the ball, what the characters are like before they are transformed by love.

1   In pairs make a list of what the audience knows about each of the characters so far.

Example

Romeo	Juliet
He has been depressed lately.	She will soon be 14.

2   It is important that Romeo enters the ball looking for Rosaline and that Juliet enters looking for Paris. This will make it clear to the audience that, when they meet, their expectations have been undercut. With your partner write a paragraph for each character outlining their thoughts and expectations as they enter the ball.

Example
Juliet: I wonder if Paris is here already ...

3   In pairs read lines 93 to 106, the first words that Romeo and Juliet speak to each other. These lines are written as a sonnet, a 14-line poem that ends with a rhyming couplet. Sonnets were very popular in Shakespeare's time, especially to express love. How might an audience react to this sonnet and this meeting? Consider:

   • What is the effect when Romeo and Juliet's lines start rhyming with each other?
   • How might the audience feel about the kiss?
   • What is the effect on the audience of the religious imagery: pilgrims, shrines and prayers?
   • How do the audience feel, knowing that they are from rival families?

Hate

1 a In pairs read through lines 54 to 92. Make a list of five character qualities of Capulet and five of Tybalt. For each one find a line from the text as evidence of that quality. This can either be something that the character says or something that is said about them.

Example
Tybalt is hot-tempered.

Tybalt	But this intrusion shall,
	Now seeming sweet, convert to bitterest gall!

b With your partner construct a freeze-frame of the moment when Capulet loses his temper with Tybalt and reminds him who is in charge.

c Discuss with your partner how each character feels about the other at this moment.

2 a Capulet knows of Romeo and thinks well of him. In pairs discuss what effect this has on the way the audience views Romeo.

b What is the effect of moving straight from Tybalt's pledge to cause trouble to Romeo and Juliet's first words to each other?

Love and hate

The short conversations between Capulet and Tybalt (lines 60 to 88), and between Romeo and Juliet (lines 93 to 110), set up the events which will take place during the rest of the play. They are important in creating the audience's expectations of what will happen next.

1 Fill in a copy of this table for the end of the scene. Place yourself in the position of each of the characters, and then of the audience.

	What they want to happen next	**What they expect to happen next**
Romeo	He wants to see Juliet again and spend time with her.	He won't see Juliet for ages because she won't want him when she finds out that he is a Montague.
Juliet		
Tybalt		
The audience		

ACT 2 SCENE 2: THE LOVE IS ESTABLISHED

Each activity in this section leads directly onto the next. However, it is possible to use any of them separately. The focus of the activities is on the characters of Romeo and Juliet and the kind of love they commit to.

CONVENTIONS DISCARDED

In this famous scene Romeo and Juliet declare their love for one another. It is a powerful scene because both characters are in an unfamiliar situation. Circumstances have prevented them from playing the conventional courtship game. To appreciate this fully it is important to consider what traditional courtship would have been like.

1　a　If Romeo were a Capulet, he would have been introduced to Juliet by her parents in the traditional way. The traditional mode of wooing for the boy would have relied on flattery. The traditional response for the girl would be to remain coy and aloof. Someone else would always have been present at their meetings. In pairs devise a ten-line scene showing what the first meeting between the lovers would have been like if Romeo were not a Montague.

　　b　How would an audience have reacted to the characters if they had been presented in this way? What do you think it is about the way that Romeo and Juliet fall in love in the play that ensures the audience is sympathetic to the characters and their plight?

THE LOVERS

1　a　In pairs read through the scene, making a note of your first impressions of Romeo and Juliet.

　　b　If you were the director, how would you want the two characters to be seen by the audience? You could look at the scene photographs on pages 96 and 97 to see some examples. Consider:

- Set: Is there a balcony? What is the effect of the two characters being on different levels? What obstacles are there in the way of Romeo physically being with Juliet?
- Staging: Which character would you place closer to the audience and why?
- Costume: Has Juliet changed into a nightgown? If so, why?

2   From the start of the scene Juliet seems more practical than Romeo.
    For example, her first speech sets out a way of resolving their
    problem: either Romeo can give up the name of Montague or she will
    give up the name of Capulet. Romeo, on the other hand, continues to
    use language full of imagery and metaphor.

    a   In pairs find five examples of this difference in the way they speak.
        One person should find five examples of Juliet's direct, practical
        speech. The other should find five examples of imagery and
        metaphor in Romeo's speech.

    b   Read through these examples. Consider:

        • What do the different ways of speaking reveal about each of the
          characters and their attitudes to love?
        • What effect might the different manners of speech have on the
          audience?

3   a   During this scene there are important moments in which Romeo
        and Juliet's relationship becomes more serious. These are usually
        when Juliet moves things forwards, for example by stating her love.
        In pairs find three such moments in this scene.

    b   Devise a freeze-frame for each of these three moments. Caption
        each one with an appropriate line from the scene, for example,
        Juliet's 'Dost thou love me?' (line 90).

    c   With your partner discuss what the response of both the other
        character and the audience might be at each moment.

    d   The frantic pace of the relationship and of the play is established in
        this scene. Do you think an audience should be aware of the speed
        or merely swept along by the tide of events?

4 a Imagery of light and darkness is very important in this play, particularly in this scene. In pairs make a list of all the references to light and darkness in the scene. One person should write out the relevant lines spoken by Romeo and the other Juliet's lines.

Example

ROMEO   The brightness of her cheek would shame those stars
As daylight doth a lamp.
(lines 19 to 20)

b What effect do you think these references to light and brightness have on the audience and the way they view the love of the young couple? What is the effect of the references to darkness?

5 a Juliet exits and then re-enters twice in this scene. In pairs read through the last few lines before each of Juliet's exits, Romeo's speech while he is alone, and the first few lines after she re-enters (lines 133 to 146, and lines 152 to 163).

b In productions this splitting of the scene into sections gives the audience the impression of the passage of time. Consider:

- What effect might this impression of time passing have on the way the audience views the relationship between Romeo and Juliet?
- Juliet's exits also show that she is at the mercy of the adults in her life. What is the effect of this on the way the audience views her character and her feelings towards Romeo?

6 a In pairs write a ten-line version of this scene. You can use either lines from Shakespeare's text or modern language. Try to highlight the differences between Romeo and Juliet and their language.

b Read through your scene. Consider:

- Do you feel that Romeo and Juliet's feelings are love or infatuation?
- How far are the emotions of the young couple driven by the freedom they feel because they are acting outside the control of their parents?

ACT 3 SCENE 1: THE FIGHT

Each activity in this section leads directly onto the next. However, it is possible to use any of them separately. The focus of the activities is on the killing of Mercutio and Tybalt and the effect of their deaths.

This scene is the turning point in the play. The first two Acts have seen Romeo and Juliet's relationship begin, their love declared and the couple married. From the moment that Romeo kills Tybalt, however, things begin to go wrong, as we knew from the Prologue that they would. This is also the scene which demonstrates the passion of the play: how unwisely people can behave when they let emotion take over. From the moment that Benvolio says 'For now, these hot days, is the mad blood stirring' (line 4) the audience is waiting for a fight to happen.

TENSION AND CONFLICT
So much changes during this scene that it is important to trace the journey of each character, particularly that of Romeo.

1 a In groups of four decide who will take the roles of the following characters: Romeo, Benvolio, Mercutio and Tybalt.

  b Discuss where each of the characters might have been immediately before this scene. What state of mind do you think each character is in as the scene begins?

  Example
  Romeo has just got married. He feels …

2 **a** In groups of four take the parts of Romeo, Benvolio, Mercutio and Tybalt. Devise a freeze-frame for each of the following lines. Some of the freeze-frames will not contain all of the characters.

- **MERCUTIO** Thou art as hot a Jack in thy mood as any in Italy (lines 11 to 12)
- **TYBALT** Mercutio, thou consortest with Romeo (line 42)
- **TYBALT** thou art a villain (line 58)
- **ROMEO** I do protest I never injured thee,
  But love thee better than thou canst devise (lines 65 to 66)
- **MERCUTIO** O calm, dishonourable, vile submission! (line 70)
- **ROMEO** Hold, Tybalt! Good Mercutio! (line 86)
- **MERCUTIO** I was hurt under your arm. (line 99)
- **BENVOLIO** O Romeo, Romeo! Brave Mercutio is dead! (line 112)
- **ROMEO** Either thou or I, or both, must go with him. (line 125)
- **ROMEO** O, I am fortune's fool! (line 132)

b In your groups work out a thought-line for each character in each of the freeze-frames above.

Example
TYBALT Mercutio, thou consortest with Romeo
Benvolio: Ignore it Mercutio, please.

c Go through the freeze-frames after Romeo has entered (freezes 3 to 10) with Romeo speaking his thoughts as one long narration.

Example
MERCUTIO O calm, dishonourable, vile submission!
Romeo: Please don't fight, Mercutio – if Tybalt is hurt while I am here, Juliet will hate me.

d Consider:

- Which moment do you think is the turning point in the scene?
- Exactly what is it that makes Romeo lose his temper?
- Do you think this loss of control is out of character for Romeo?
- Could anything have prevented Romeo from responding in this way?

3 a In groups of four take the parts of Romeo, Benvolio, Mercutio and Tybalt. Use the lines listed above in part **2a** as a shortened version of the scene. Act this out, trying to capture the urgency and the pace of events. What do you think it is that gives an 'unstoppable' feeling to this scene?

b In a few productions the director has decided to add in the character of 'Fate', or a chorus of women representing fate, as in a Greek play. Choose one moment from the scene when you think that having such a character or characters would be useful, and decide what they could do at this point in the scene.

Examples
- 'Fate' could push Romeo in front of Mercutio so that Mercutio is killed under Romeo's arm.
- 'Fate' could pick up the sword of the dead Mercutio and hand it to Romeo.

THE REPORTING OF EVENTS

1 a Read through lines 137 to 193, from the entrance of the Prince. Make a list of what each of the following characters wants: the Prince, Capulet, Lady Capulet, Montague, Lady Montague, and Benvolio.

Example
Lady Capulet wants the Prince to sentence Romeo to death.

b In this section of the scene which character does the audience have most sympathy with? Why?

c The Prince ends the scene by saying 'Mercy but murders, pardoning those that kill' (line 193). What do you think about his judgement?

2 In pairs write a press statement from the Prince following this scene. Consider:

- How important is it that the Prince is seen to be neutral in the feud?
- How far do you think he achieves this?
- What image do you think he wants to portray to his people?
- How does he feel personally about the loss of his kinsman, Mercutio?

ACT 3 SCENES 2 AND 3: REACTIONS TO THE NEWS OF BANISHMENT

Each activity in this section leads directly onto the next. However, it is possible to use any of them separately. The focus of the activities is on how Romeo and Juliet respond to Romeo's banishment, and the roles of the Friar and Nurse.

The responses of Romeo and Juliet to the news of Romeo's banishment set in motion the events which follow and set up the way in which the young couple and the audience view their relationship. These two scenes run parallel to each other, clearly showing the differences between Juliet and Romeo as well as the parallel roles of the Friar and the Nurse as trusted friends to them.

THE JOURNEY OF JULIET AND ROMEO

1   a   In pairs go through Act 3 Scene 2 and make a list of all of the important things that happen or are talked about.

Example
   • Juliet waits impatiently for Romeo.
   • The Nurse enters and throws down the rope-ladder.

   b   Go through Act 3 Scene 3 and make a list of all of the important things that happen or are talked about.

Example
   • Romeo is called in by the Friar.
   • The Friar tells Romeo he is banished.

   c   With your partner one person should read out the list of events for Act 3 Scene 2 one at a time. After each one the other person, taking the role of Juliet, should step forwards and say what she is thinking at that point. Then you should swap roles and do the same for Act 3 Scene 3 with one of you taking the role of Romeo.

Example
   • Juliet waits impatiently for Romeo.
      Juliet: Come on, Romeo – where are you?

d Repeat the exercise in part **c**. When the person playing Romeo or Juliet steps forwards to speak their thought, this time the size of the step should reflect how greatly the character is affected by that event. For example, you might think that Juliet should take a big step (i.e. is very affected) when the Nurse criticises Romeo. Discuss with your partner what you think has the most effect on the characters of Romeo and Juliet and why.

e Repeat the exercise in part d, but this time the size of the step should reflect whether or not the character changes greatly as a result of the event. For example, you might think that Juliet should take a big step (i.e. changes a lot) as she realises that her loyalty must lie with her husband.

f Which of the characters changes most in these scenes? Consider:

- In what different ways do each of the characters respond to the news of Romeo's banishment?
- How has this further obstacle affected the desire and determination of each character to be together?
- Which of the characters has demonstrated most maturity and independence?

THE NURSE AND FRIAR LAWRENCE

1 In pairs improvise a short scene which shows what happens between Juliet and the Nurse in Act 3 Scene 2. Think about what is most important about their relationship and how the status and dependence within the relationship is changing. You can include some dialogue but should concentrate on actions rather than words. Consider:

- What qualities is it most important for the Nurse to have?
- How do you think the Nurse should look, move and behave?
- What feelings do Juliet and the Nurse have for one another?

Example
You could begin the scene with Juliet running to the window two or three times to see if the Nurse is coming.

2 Improvise a scene to show what happens between Romeo and the Friar in Act 3 Scene 3. Think about what is most important about their relationship and how the status and dependence within the relationship is changing. You can include some dialogue but should concentrate on actions rather than words. Consider:

- How long do you think that the Friar has been a friend to Romeo?
- How old would you want the Friar to be?
- How would he move and behave?

Example
You could begin the scene with the Friar calling to Romeo, in order to give him the important news.

3 a In pairs, one person considering the Friar and the other the Nurse, make a list of words which describe:

- their character
- their relationship with Juliet/Romeo
- their function in the play
- how the audience feel about them

Example
The Nurse's character is bawdy, loud, busy, warm …

b Discuss the similarities and differences between the roles of the Nurse and the Friar in the play, based on the lists you have made. Consider:

- What difference does it make that the Friar is a holy man?
- Are we more likely to trust his judgement because of his faith?
- How far do you think the Nurse takes on a maternal role?
- How much difference does it make that the Nurse seems to be the only friend of Juliet while Romeo has many friends of his own age as well as the Friar?

ACT 5 SCENE 3: THE DEATHS

Each activity in this section leads directly onto the next. However, it is possible to use any of them separately. The focus is on the final journeys of Romeo and Juliet and the impact of their deaths.

The desire to know what happens next holds the attention of an audience in any play. The final scene of this play is full of opportunities and events that could change the course of the action, so that an audience, despite knowing what the final outcome will be, is gripped to the end.

LOST OPPORTUNITIES

1 **a** In pairs read through lines 1 to 170, the point at which both Romeo and Juliet are dead. Make a list of all the things that could have occurred to prevent their deaths.

   Example
   Paris could have stopped Romeo from entering the tomb.

   b Using your list discuss with your partner how you think the audience feels each time an opportunity for the lovers to be saved is presented and then removed.

THE DEATHS OF THE LOVERS

1 **a** In pairs read through the lines leading to the deaths of Romeo and Juliet, lines 85 to 120, and 148 to 170.

   b If you were the director, how would you want to stage this scene in order to make it moving and powerful? You could look at the photographs on pages 256 and 257 to see some examples. Consider:

   • How gruesome would you want the vault to be? Remember that Romeo and Juliet are viewed in contrast to their surroundings.
   • What kind of lighting effects would you want to use?
   • How would you position the lovers when they are dead?
   • Would you have music at any point in the scene?
   • How important is the timing of the deaths? For example, in some productions Juliet begins to stir after Romeo has taken the poison, but before he dies. In a few productions, he sees her move and realises she is not dead, but it is too late. When would you want Juliet to wake?

2 The audience is usually on the side of the lovers, willing them to find a way to be together. In some productions the audience are left with the impression that Romeo and Juliet will somehow be together in another world after death; perhaps death is just one more obstacle that they must overcome. This impression is reinforced by the numerous references to the stars, fate and light through the play.

   a In pairs consider the moment of Juliet's death, as she finally takes her place beside her husband. Devise a freeze-frame for this moment.

   b Caption this freeze-frame with what you would want the audience to be thinking and feeling at this moment.

3 After the deaths of Romeo and Juliet the Friar's speech (lines 229 to 269) leads the audience to look more objectively at the feud. Remember that the audience knew from the Prologue that the Capulets and the Montagues would, through the deaths of their children, finally put aside their grudge.

   a In pairs go through the last scene and make a list of the lines which put the deaths of Romeo and Juliet into this wider context.

     Examples

     FR. LAWRENCE A greater power than we can contradict
                     Hath thwarted our intents. Come, come away!
                     (lines 153 to 154)

     CAPULET   Poor sacrifices of our enmity! **(line 304)**

   b Discuss the effect these lines might have on the audience. Consider:

     • How might an audience feel about the feud by the end of the play?

     • Will the peace between the two families be more important to the audience now than it was before the love and deaths of Romeo and Juliet?

     • How might an audience feel about fate or destiny at the end of the play? Has it been a positive or negative driving force, do you think?